Lactation Private Practice

From Start to Strong

Annie Frisbie, IBCLC, MA

Published by Annie Frisbie IBCLC, Inc., PO Box 5731, Astoria, NY 11105, paperlesslactation.com

Printed on acid-free paper.

Annie Frisbie IBCLC, Inc. 2019

First Edition

Copyediting by Brian J. White
Photos by Laura Vladimirova, bebebirthphotography.com

"It is easier to build strong children than to repair broken men."

—Frederick Douglass

"Only when our clever brain and our human heart work together in harmony can we achieve our true potential."

—Jane Goodall

"Then Moses's sister said to Pharaoh's daughter, 'Shall I go and call you a nurse from the Hebrew women to nurse the child for you?' And Pharaoh's daughter said to her, 'Go.' So the girl went and called the Moses's mother. And Pharaoh's daughter said to her, 'Take this child away and nurse him for me, and I will give you your wages.' So the woman took [her] child and nursed him."

—Exodus 2:7-8 (ESV)

To Frances, Teba, and Cathy, who brought me into La Leche League and changed the course of my life in ways that blessed me beyond measure.

To Nina, Jenn, Avi, and Cori—together we made a difference through La Leche League of Queens and you are in my heart forever.

To John, Bea, and Cora—the three of you are everything to me and all of this is for you.

CONTENTS

FOREWORD

By Jen Deshaies, IBCLC, CD, LLLL

When you are an International Board Certified Lactation Consultant (IBCLC), people are very curious about how you ended up in this line of work, and it's a topic I love talking about. I've taken numerous phone calls over the years from people who want to become an IBCLC. Past clients, La Leche League (LLL) Leaders from all over the country, medical professionals, friends of friends wanting to switch careers, and more have asked how to get started the lactation field. Each phone call reminds me why I love IBCLC work so deeply and passionately, but after I hang up I often wonder if I've given a balanced perspective of my career.

Ten years ago I was pregnant with my first child and had a government job. I never once considered working in maternal health. I often tell my daughter that her birth and our breastfeeding relationship was my initial inspiration, but it was still years before I knew I needed to be an IBCLC. About a month before I was accredited as a La Leche League Leader a childhood friend needed help with her non-latching newborn. I offered to stop by and help her, and I was thrilled when she said yes. On the drive back home I remember calling my best friend and saying *"THIS* is what I am meant to do." The pure exhilaration of helping a new mom in person was something I'd never felt so intensely before in my life.

Over the next few years I soaked up everything I could as I worked towards the IBCLC exam requirements. I became a birth and postpartum doula and began to develop experience working with clients and running a business. I also helped to grow my LLL group while establishing community connections. I learned through my LLL volunteer work by running meetings and taking helping calls, through reading textbooks and research studies, and through the online and in-person conferences I was attending. It was exhilarating to be working towards something so meaningful. I quickly developed a new vision for my life, and would find myself telling people: "My goal is to improve breastfeeding support in Syracuse, New York, over the next 30 years."

I found out I passed my IBCLC exam at the end of October 2014. It felt like I'd been waiting for this moment forever, but when it finally came, I didn't have a plan. My only option locally was private practice as I had no medical degree (which was an essential qualification listed on every IBCLC job posting). But I had very little knowledge of what I would need to do to make that happen. In those first years I charted by paper, and had no ability to fax or take credit cards. I would spend so long on doctor's reports that after a while I was utterly unmotivated to do them at all. I had little understanding of superbills and insurance. As a result, I got organized very slowly and even with a low volume of clients I felt overwhelmed by all the business-related tasks. Even so, I was seeing truly inspiring results with my clients and getting more referrals. The care I was providing was working for them—they were meeting and exceeding their own breastfeeding goals—but it was challenging for me.

I often gave my clients endless follow-up. There was little definition between my work life and personal life, and my relationships and self-care practices suffered. The satisfaction I found in my work was addicting, but the combination of my empathetic nature and inefficient practices created an unsustainable situation—both emotionally and financially. My clients were thriving, but my ratio of work to income was completely out of balance. I also recognized that I was in a position to pursue my dream career because of the support of my family. Without my husband's stable income, benefits, and support, it would have been extremely difficult to take years building my business.

As I dug deeper into complicated breastfeeding situations, I longed for a mentor. I joined Facebook groups and traveled to conferences all over the northeastern United States in search of deepening my skills and business. I began to connect with other private practice IBCLCs and discovered that so many were struggling with the same issues, but many were successful. Finding out that others were making a living doing my dream job inspired me, yet at this point I truly had to face reality: I have to make a living at this, or I have to move on.

It finally became clear to me that I needed more guidance to change my mindset, set boundaries, get organized, and work towards creating a sustainable business. The connections I was making in-person and online began to serve unknowingly as my collective mentors (and in some cases, true friends). I have found so much generosity in the lactation community, and I always try to pay that forward because it's meant so much to me. Inspired by other private practice IBCLCs that were making it work, I decided to make changes.

I wish I had understood sooner that setting boundaries and limits from the beginning would have meant helping even more families. I was meeting a huge need in my community, but I was beginning to see that I could meet that need more effectively if I put my focus on growing my business instead of giving too much away. Making this shift has been hard work. Private practice is not easy, and I wish someone had told me that before I started.

When someone calls me now asking about becoming a private practice IBCLC, I don't just focus on how gratifying it is to support clients in reaching their goals and seeing the difference that makes in their parenting, health, and lives. I also tell them that having a private practice can be a complicated career that takes a lot of energy and drive. You have to love breastfeeding, but you also have to want to be self-employed, figure out billing and insurance, learn all about HIPAA, and spend time on marketing. I don't hold back when I tell them that while I truly love what I do, almost daily I wonder if I can continue.

What motivates me to keep wading through the unknown so I can continue seeing clients? I know that for me, it's because being an IBCLC is a passion. I would tell them that if they have that passion then they are on the right path, even though it's a hard one. If they have helped a friend with breastfeeding and felt that rush of satisfaction, if they have nursed their own baby and experienced that milk-drunk oxytocin surge that feels like nothing else in the world and want to help others feel that too, then I tell them to go for it. I also tell them to be smart and strategic about starting their business the right way from the start—but that if and when they make mistakes and need to make changes, it's never too late.

Our world is desperately in need of us—the ones with so much passion that we can't sit back and *not* open our own private practice, even when we know that it will be hard work. This may be your dream job, just like it was mine—take that and run with it. Make it work. Families need you. We need you.

INTRODUCTION

The last time I checked, "lactation consultant" was not one of the careers you can choose in the game of Life. You probably didn't have it presented to you as an option when you were looking at colleges or choosing a major. You haven't dreamed of doing this since you were a child (unless perhaps your parent was one of the pioneers of our profession and you caught the vision early). In fact, finding any information at all about becoming a lactation consultant and making it work as a viable business can be very hard to come by.

For those of us working in private practice, we know that it can be isolating at times. Sure, there are great Facebook groups for support and networking, but the day-to-day reality is that your private practice rests on your shoulders alone. It can be hard to identify weaknesses or inefficiencies in your practice, and even harder to find the time to make necessary changes.

This book aims to walk you through all aspects of being a private practice IBCLC, from becoming an IBCLC through taking your business to the places of your dreams. If you are any one of the following, this book is for you:

- A student interested in providing healthcare for women, lactating persons, and/or babies, but not necessarily wanting to become a nurse or a doctor
- A breastfeeding peer counselor wanting to move into paid lactation work
- A doula, midwife, or RN looking to add additional services to their perinatal or postpartum work
- A person in an entirely different field now looking for a more family-friendly career
- Anyone who finds lactation endlessly fascinating and wonders if it could be a job

- An aspiring IBCLC studying for the exam or waiting for exam results
- A hospital IBCLC considering the switch to private practice
- A newly minted IBCLC launching a private practice
- An IBCLC currently in private practice looking for strategies to grow and expand

This book has everything you need to know about how private practice works so that you can put your skills, education, training, and (most importantly) passion to work serving breastfeeding/chestfeeding families.

ABOUT ME

December 2007. My first daughter was three weeks old and hadn't had a wet diaper in 24 hours. I was mega engorged and in so much pain. She was crying and crying and crying and we were absolutely panicked. From the dim recesses of memory filtering through the fog and chaos of my postpartum brain, I remembered what I learned in the prenatal breastfeeding class I took with Leigh Anne O'Connor and issued a command to my husband: "Call La Leche League and tell them we need help!"

Just a few hours later I was sitting on a comfy couch in an apartment in Woodhaven, Queens, using a hospital-grade pump and watching the container collect almost eight ounces of milk from my right breast alone. I was astonished at what my body could do without me even knowing it.

When my IBCLC, Catherine Watson Genna, told me that my baby was probably tongue-tied and that's why I had scabs on my nipples and pain with every feeding, I cried. Everyone else, including my wonderful homebirth midwife, had told me that breastfeeding was going to hurt a little in the beginning. Cathy referred me to Dr. Elizabeth "Betty" Coryllos, who released her tongue tie. She latched without pain immediately after, and breastfeeding never hurt again.

When my daughter was 15 months old, I completed the training to become an accredited La Leche League Leader, volunteering with our local group in Sunnyside, Queens, on the western edge of the most diverse borough in New York City. I led monthly support groups and enrichment meetings, and put in countless hours on the phone providing breastfeeding support, all while watching my daughter grow from a fat and happy and busy baby into an energetic and mobile toddler. She weaned at two years, five months, when I was seven months pregnant with her sister.

My younger daughter was also born at home, and breastfeeding was easy right from the start. In fact, she was already gaining when

3

we went to the pediatrician for her first office visit at three days old. It never hurt, she had so many wet and dirty diapers that we stopped counting early on, and the laid-back position meant that my older daughter could be close to both of us during all that constant feeding on the couch.

I was studying hard to take the IBLCE exam in July of 2011, and soaking up every word. I knew my younger daughter had a tongue tie as well, but Dr. Coryllos was no longer in practice, and because I wasn't having any problems I didn't go see Cathy again. Instead, I asked my pediatrician to refer me to an ENT, and I bet you can guess what happened next. The ENT said that she did have a "slight" tie but that he wouldn't release it until she was four months old and could go under general anesthesia. Because she was gaining so well, I figured she was one of the lucky ones whose tie wasn't going to bother her.

Cut to six weeks later. I'm in Las Vegas for my cousin's wedding. When I bought the tickets, I was remembering how easy things were when my older daughter was two months old. I could breastfeed her anywhere. I assumed it would be the same with her younger sister, or even easier since I'd already done it once before.

I couldn't have been more wrong.

Instead of attending the ceremony, I'm in my hotel room with my younger daughter. She is crying. She has been crying for weeks now, crying every moment she is awake. Every time she is hungry, it's the same thing. I try to breastfeed her and she cries, screams, turns her head away, turns back, turns away again. I pick her up and bounce her and try again. I change positions. I walk around. Eventually, after about 20 minutes, she wears herself out crying and falls asleep. I keep her on me because I know after about 5-10 minutes she will latch on in her sleep. She is gaining beautifully and I'm not needing to use any bottles, but she is miserable and I'm exhausted and it feels like our whole family is falling apart.

I sent Cathy an email saying that I thought maybe I had oversupply or something, and she kindly suggested I come in to see her. Cathy explained how even a so-called "slight" tongue tie can trigger a nursing strike. An occupational therapist named Diklah Barak was working with Cathy at the time and they taught me strategies to manage the nursing strike while also dealing with the tongue tie.

I ended up taking my daughter to see an ENT who would do frenotomies without general anesthesia, and was grateful that it was covered by insurance. But unlike before, things didn't get better right away. When we were still involved in the same feeding drama by four months, we went back to the ENT for a second revision. Finally, when she was five-and-a-half months old, I was able to nurse her while she was awake and we were in a public place (the New York Hall of Science under-five room). I can still summon that feeling of relief years later. She went on to nurse until the day of her first ballet recital, the week before she turned five.

Passing the IBCLE exam in 2011 was a high point in my life. I've always pursued challenges and new experiences, but this work felt different. It was the first time I'd experienced a sense of calling. When coupled with my volunteer work as a LLL Leader, I truly felt like I was making a difference in the world.

Before becoming an IBCLC, I had had a lot of different jobs and career paths, with the only unifying thread being that I've almost always been a freelancer. I've been a screenwriter (*Speak* starring Kristen Stewart was my first baby), a movie critic, a screenwriting professor, and a blogger on the intersection of tech and media. I spent several years in film production, first as assistant to several different movie producers who had me performing jobs that ranged from going to the dry cleaners to pick up laundry to going to the airport to pick up movie stars. I also was a product placement and clearance coordinator for a bunch of movies including *Far From Heaven*, a film I consider a masterpiece.

I loved the energy and excitement and craziness of film work, but once I became pregnant with my older daughter, I knew I wanted to be with her and not on set. I turned my attention back to writing and kept that going while working on qualifying for the IBLCE exam. I was hired to write a few screenplays that never made it out of development, and one screenplay that did (*The Good Witch's Destiny* for Hallmark).

As my private practice grew, my opportunities to continue writing movies seemed to be fading, but it felt right to me to embrace the transition. After all, working with new families means working with stories, but instead of being the one writing the story, I'm the one watching the story unfold. And every family's story is so completely different it astonishes me. I am truly grateful that this work has come into my life.

Like many of you, I struggle with the ebbs and flows of private practice IBCLC work. I have times when the phone doesn't ring, and times when I'm turning people away. I've oscillated between giving unlimited follow-up to creating a "no phone calls" policy. I'm juggling work and family and sometimes all the balls are on the floor. And in all of that, I'm working hard to understand my own privilege and how that contributes to inequities in healthcare so that I can be an ally and work towards justice in our profession and for the families we serve. Sound familiar?

I wrote this book not only to help you establish your private practice as an IBCLC, but also because I want you to thrive in private practice. By creating a sound business structure, you'll have the support you need to give your clients the care and compassion that our work requires. You don't need to piece it together or build it from scratch, you can start out right and that's what will make you strong.

How to Use this Book

In these pages, you will find a blueprint towards creating the IBCLC private practice that will allow you to thrive.

This book is written for all IBCLCs; however, many of the recommendations are specific to the United States.

I use the term "client" to refer to the primary breastfeeding/chestfeeding parent, not "patient" as in the medical world, because lactation is not an illness, it's a fundamental biological process and a key component of wellness for parent and baby. When I provide resources from the medical world that use the term "patient," please understand that to be the equivalent of "client" for the purposes of this book.

Not all lactating persons identify as female, so throughout this book I will use the gender-neutral pronouns "they" and "them." For ease of readability, "breastfeeding" will be used throughout and also encompasses chestfeeding. The accepted term when charting the examination of the breastfeeding parent is the gendered term "maternal" and because charts may be subject to external review in case of an audit or legal action, this term remains appropriate for your internal use.

If you are not yet an IBCLC, this book is not a substitute for any of the lactation education required to pass the IBLCE exam, and is designed to point you towards deeper study in these areas.

In each section, I've compiled a list of curated resources designed to help you dive deeper and increase your understanding and skills. If you're reading the print version of this book, you can find these resources on my website at paperlesslactation.com/private-practice-resources using the password PAPERBACK.

Some of my resources are affiliate links, meaning I will receive a financial benefit if you purchase through my link. When linking to a book or a service, if you prefer not to use my affiliate link, simply search for the book or service without going through my link. The links I provide do not imply endorsement of any advertising or paid services that may appear on any web page hosting an article I recommend.

Because there is a dearth of IBCLC-specific resources pertaining to business and legal issues, I will be linking to some articles for psychotherapists. Their ethical standards for privacy exceed ours, so following their best practices will more than meet the IBLCE Code of Professional Conduct.

Full disclosure: I am the author of *Paperless Private Practice for Lactation Consultants*, and will be referring to it throughout. Not only that, but I'll be recommending you buy it and my related products and services, and will earn money if you do. I am not an attorney, but this book was reviewed thoroughly by my attorney.

WHAT IS AN IBCLC?

An IBCLC is a lactation consultant who has achieved the highest level of training within the field of lactation, and is "a healthcare professional who specializes in the clinical management of breastfeeding," according to the International Lactation Consultant Association (ILCA). But isn't breastfeeding normal and natural? Why on earth do we need someone to tell us how to do it? Because support with the initiation and continuation of breastfeeding is how families across cultures have been able to reach their goals.

IBCLC stands for International Board Certified Lactation Consultant. This certification is issued by the International Board of Lactation Consultant Examiners (IBLCE). An IBCLC has completed a rigorous education, performed supervised clinical hours, and has passed an examination given by the IBLCE.

An IBCLC is required to re-certify every five years by taking the exam or by submitting proof of continuing education. There are many other kinds of helpers in the breastfeeding landscape, some of whom call themselves "lactation consultants," and this is very confusing for families. Using the term IBCLC when describing our work is an important form of advocacy for the highest level of professional standards in non-medical lactation-specific healthcare.

IBCLCs work with families who are breastfeeding or chestfeeding. These services are provided in hospitals, in an office setting (either freestanding or associated with a medical practice), and in the family's home. The private-practice IBCLC performs home visits and/or working out of an office. Private practice means they are not affiliated with a hospital, clinic, or medical practice. In addition to individual services, the IBCLC may offer group drop-in clinics or support groups, hold prenatal classes, and provide training and mentorship to aspiring IBCLCs. IBCLCs often sell or rent supplies like hospital-grade pumps, at-breast supplementers, and baby scales, to name a few. Some IBCLCs are in-network with insurance companies; most IBCLCs accept payment at the time of service. All IBCLCs are expected to adhere to the IBLCE Code of Professional Conduct.

At the time of writing, only a handful of states have passed bills licensing lactation consultants. This means that many hospital or outpatient jobs for lactation consultants may require you to have a medical license (such as Registered Nurse) in order to qualify for employment. For private practice, you do not need a medical license, but you will be dealing with consumer confusion over the myriad types of lactation support credentials, and potentially competing with people offering a lower standard of support but still using the title "lactation consultant." There's room at the table for all kinds of breastfeeding helpers. We all have a valuable role to play towards increasing breastfeeding initiation rates and duration, but you may need to spend time educating your community on the value of the IBCLC.

The United States has a law in called the Affordable Care Act (ACA), still in effect at the time of this book's publication. A key provision is that lactation services are labeled as preventive, meaning that theoretically insurance companies must cover such services 100 percent with no cost-sharing for the patient. The common forms of cost-sharing are:

- Co-pays, where the client must pay a set dollar amount to the provider at the time of the visit
- Co-insurance, where the client is responsible for a percentage (usually low) of the payment to the provider
- Deductible, where the client must spend a certain amount of money on healthcare before services are paid for

Lactation services are exempt from all of these kinds of fees under the Affordable Care Act, but in reality, many insurance companies are putting up substantial roadblocks for families to access this benefit; mainly, they are requiring that services be performed by a licensed provider. Since standalone IBCLCs are not licensed in most states, that can prevent families from getting our services reimbursed. This affects underserved populations disproportionately, who may only have access to lactation care through the medical system. Some insurance plans are exempt from ACA regulations through a process known as "grandfathering," where they were not required to adopt ACA provision because their existence predated the ACA. These clients will never get reimbursement.

Insurance companies may also say, "sure, we'll cover it, but you have to see an in-network provider." If they can provide an in-network provider, great. But in many cases, there may be no in-network provider for hundreds of miles, or there is an in-network provider, but they are not available. When this happens, the Affordable Care Act is very clear that insurance companies should pre-authorize an out-of-network provider and reimburse the client. This is sometimes called "gap coverage" or "in/out coverage" or "out-of-network exemption." It often requires that the client contact the insurance company in advance and obtain a pre-authorization. Individual payers may have their own internal term (Blue Cross/Blue Shield calls it "Level One Review)." Encourage clients to call their insurance before the visit to increase the likelihood that their carrier will comply with the ACA.

A sad truth is that many insurance companies are still denying claims despite the ACA. Often, what happens is that the claim will be denied by the insurance company, and the client will need to go through the appeals process in order to access their full benefits under the law. This can be an arduous and frustrating process for your clients, requiring empathy and encouragement from you—but not direct communication with the insurance company. When you are out-of-network, you are not contracted with the insurance company. If they call you, do not discuss client details over the phone and only release client files with a written request from the insurance company and the express permission of the client. Your client needs to fight this fight with their insurance company; you will support your clients. The National Women's Law Center offers excellent resources for families on accessing full benefits under the ACA.

The IBCLC:

- What is an IBCLC?
- International Board of Lactation Consultant Examiners
- IBLCE Certification FAQs
- IBLCE Code of Professional Conduct
- The Alphabet Soup of Breastfeeding Support
- IBCLC vs. CLC – which is better? Why are we asking?

Why IBCLCs matter:

- Secrets Of Breastfeeding From Global Moms In The Know
- Breastfeeding in Underserved Women: Increasing Initiation and Continuation of Breastfeeding
- What Is Chestfeeding?

Licensure in the USA:

- Licensure for IBCLCs FAQ
- Licensing the IBCLC

The Affordable Care Act (USA):

- How Does the Affordable Care Act Impact Breastfeeding Families?
- Breastfeeding Benefits: Understanding Your Coverage Under the Affordable Care Act
- I Know All About The ACA's Breastfeeding Benefit, and I Couldn't Get Services Covered

Essential IBCLC Reading:

- International Code of Marketing of Breast-milk Substitutes

- <u>Innocenti Declaration: On the Protection, Promotion and Support of Breastfeeding</u>
- <u>Baby-friendly Hospital Initiative</u>

PREPARING FOR IBCLC PRIVATE PRACTICE

There are three key components to IBCLC private practice to understand when approaching this decision. The first is that you will be a healthcare provider, serving people who are often feeling anxious, overwhelmed, and even afraid. The second is that you will be an entrepreneur, running a business with the goal of supporting yourself and your family. Finally, you must meet or exceed the Clinical Competencies for the Practice of IBCLCs.

When asking yourself whether or not you have what it takes to enter any profession, use future-focused thinking in order to evaluate your potential for success in the field. This self-assessment is not about where you are right now, but what you believe you can become. So when you read these sections, don't ask "Am I good at this skill?" Instead, ask, "Am I excited to learn more about this skill?"

A seed, in and of itself, isn't good at growing—in fact, if left alone with only its own innate qualities, nothing at all will happen. It will stay a seed. But if a seed gets the right kind of input (sun, water), within the right context (appropriate climate), and receives the necessary care (cultivation), it will achieve and even surpass its full potential.

The seed is you. The context is private practice as an IBCLC. Later chapters of this book will delve deep into cultivating your practice. But first, let's explore the input you'll need to give your seed—clinical skills, business skills, and staying power skills. If what you read here excites you and motivates you to want to learn, grow, and thrive in the climate of IBCLC private practice, then this may truly be the work you are meant to do.

Before delving into a discussion of the skills needed for private practice, it is important to point out that there are barriers to developing these skills, some of which may be significant. Qualifying for the exam requires both financial resources—to pay for education materials, the fee for the exam, and costs associated accruing supervised clinical hours—and access to an appropriate setting in which to perform the supervised clinical hours.

It's the second that can prove most daunting for aspiring lactation consultants in underserved communities. Perhaps there are no other IBCLCs in your area, for example if you live in a rural setting or if your community lacks representation within the greater local IBCLC community. You may also be wondering how to afford to be able to essentially work for free while gaining the supervised clinical hours. If you do not have children that you breastfed, some of the volunteer organizations may not be an option for you.

At the time of this writing, these issues are still very much unresolved. There is a growing awareness of the ways in which systemic racism contribute to inequities in maternal and infant mortality rates, and voices which interrogate privilege and advocate for change are gaining in influence. While these advances are welcome and necessary, they are only the beginning. Much more work needs to be done to change the paradigm and open up more opportunities for applicants from underserved communities to become IBCLCs.

If you are reading this book and feeling shut out of the profession because of your race, ethnicity, gender identity, economic status, or anything else, first let me say that I hear you and I believe you. Your struggle is real and valid and represents a crisis for our profession. I encourage you to share your story, not only to be heard, but also to leverage the power of social media and the collegiality of the IBCLC community to aid you in reaching your goals and provoke necessary changes in the structures of our profession.

- Clinical Competencies for the Practice of IBCLCs
- <u>Barriers to the IBCLC Profession</u>
- <u>Reaching Our Sisters Everywhere (ROSE)</u>
- <u>Seven Ways to Support Black Breastfeeding Week</u>

-
-
-
-
-

Clinical Skills

Your clinical skills encompass everything you need to do in order to perform the client-sided tasks of private practice. You must adhere to the IBLCE Code of Professional Conduct and stay within the Scope of Practice for IBCLCs. You will develop these skills during your education and training to become an IBCLC.

Before going into detail about the different kinds of clinical skills you'll need to cultivate, it's important to understand that lactation work is much more complicated than it may appear at first. It's never just a bad latch, or low milk supply, or what that hospital nurse may have called a "lazy baby." The situations we deal with are often multifactorial, involving a commingling of factors that are interrelated and inseparable.

For example, that bad latch is from a tongue tie, but because the family waited so long to see you, that tongue tie gave the baby an inefficient suck that drove the milk supply down. Will releasing the tongue tie bring the milk supply up? Not without giving the parent instructions on expressing milk. The family is going to need instruction and counseling on what to do after the tongue tie is released in order to help the baby achieve full oral function.

Far too often, we will hear that a family in this kind of situation will be told, "just work on the latch" or "there's always formula," and we cringe inside. We know our clients have not been given the appropriate tools—or even told there are any tools at all. They may believe that they need to try harder, or assume that there is something wrong with them. If they're also dealing with birth trauma, postpartum depression, or a history of sexual abuse, the language their doctors use may be triggering and prevent them from acting on recommendations. Our clients of color face the reality that being born African-American puts you at greater risk of dying in childbirth or in the postpartum period, and that your baby is more likely to die in infancy even with good healthcare and nutrition. We bring all of this complexity to our interactions, which are always, *always* about more than just the mechanics of a latch.

In other words, there isn't a decision tree we can follow that says "if this... then do this..." to fix breastfeeding problems. Each dyad has a story, and only time, attention, training, and deep listening will reveal the appropriate path to wellness specific to that situation. We're more like relationship therapists than anything else, guiding two (or more) people into a healthy equilibrium that's mutually beneficial for both and ideally allows each to achieve their fullest potential in their given role.

The best IBCLCs I know are always learning, growing, questioning, seeking, and evolving—if that excites you, read on.

- IBLCE Code of Professional Conduct
- Scope of Practice for IBCLCs
- <u>Every Patient Tells a Story by Lisa Sanders</u>
- <u>Clinical Competencies for the Practice of IBCLCs</u>
- <u>What is a clinical skill? Searching for order in chaos through a modified Delphi process</u>
- <u>Clinical Skills in the Undergraduate Medical Curriculum: A Road Map</u>

Physical Examination Skills

When we work with a breastfeeding dyad (or multiples), we are using most of our senses in order to assess what is happening physically with both the parent and the baby. I haven't yet used my sense of taste in private practice (and I feel this is an appropriate limit to set for myself), but I have used all the others:

- Sight: looking with my eyes at the anatomy of parent and baby, and watching what happens when they come together at the breast
- Hearing: listening to sucks and swallows and other sounds made by the baby during feeding
- Smell: experiencing the odor of gas or stool produced by the baby that signal digestive upset
- Touch: using my hands to examine the parent's breasts and to perform an oral examination inside the baby's mouth

Developing these skills requires finding an in-person mentor. If you are working towards your exam qualifications as a recognized peer counselor or a licensed medical professional, it is possible to meet the exam requirements without ever having touched a mother's breasts or performed on oral exam on a baby. These skills are critical in private practice, and I recommend seeking out opportunities for hands-on learning even if technically you don't need them in order to take the exam. You will not be effective in private practice without being skilled in physically examining both parent and baby.

It is also vitally important to understand that both parent and baby have the right to consent to being touched. A parent can respond verbally when asked, "May I have permission to touch your breasts?" In most cases, the parent will say yes, but there are some situations where you will not be permitted to touch. A baby cannot respond verbally, but will give nonverbal cues that signal if they are amenable to having a gloved finger placed in their mouths. It is very important that we know how to read and interpret the cues given to us by the baby, and that we respect their autonomy over their own bodies.

Questions for self-reflection:

- Do I have time and/or resources to commit to learning how to perform a physical assessment of both parent and baby?
- Do I respect the right of a person over their own body, and am I willing to learn how infants communicate consent to be touched?
- Can I find the time and the resources to work with a mentor to learn hands-on assessment skills? (If access is an issue, read the section above.)

Recommended resources:

- Breastfeeding and Human Lactation, Enhanced 5th Edition
- Breastfeeding: A Guide for the Medical Profession
- Informed Consent FAQs

Critical Thinking and Procedural Knowledge

"Help! My 2-week old baby is so fussy when breastfeeding. What do I do?" You know what happens next when a version of this question gets posted on social media—within 15 minutes there will be a zillion replies, none of them the same!

- "Hang in there, sounds normal. Just nurse on demand."
- "My sister had to do a full elimination diet and only ate turkey and squash for a year because her baby was so fussy. But maybe try cutting out dairy."
- "Sounds like reflux, ask your pediatrician for Zantac."
- "My nanny recommended gripe water and it saved our lives."
- "Could it be tongue tie? Maybe if you post a picture we can check for you."

- "Your baby is hungry! I didn't have enough milk but didn't realize my baby was starving. As soon as I gave formula things got better #fedisbest."
- "It's a wonder week."
- "It's a growth spurt."
- "Hold your baby more."
- "Don't hold your baby so much."
- "Thrush."

So which is it? The answer is one, some, none, or all of the above. It takes critical thinking—defined as "the objective analysis and evaluation of an issue in order to form a judgment"—to figure out what exactly is going on with your clients and their babies and make appropriate recommendations. You are making decisions based on your interpretation of the data you are gathering with your senses while taking the intake and health history and during the physical examination.

Once you have determined the root cause of the issue at hand, you are using procedural knowledge—defined as "knowledge exercised in the performance of some task"—to educate and counsel your clients in the appropriate course of action. You are not relying on one-size-fits-all protocols or handouts, you are developing personalized care. For example, you'll know when a baby needs to be supplemented at each feeding, and you'll know when a baby may just need a few ounces to turn the situation around. You'll know when to recommend a hospital-grade pump, and when to tell the family to put the pump away. If you are recommending the use of a device, you know how to use it and how to explain its use to the family.

In the beginning, you may find your thinking processes to be systematic, a calculated process of evaluation and decision-making. You may need to make lists, or charts, or diagrams; you may stay up late rereading textbooks or emailing with your mentor. Your intuition is a muscle, and with every client you see you have the opportunity to make it stronger by asking questions and looking closely. As you get a critical mass of clients under your belt, you'll find that your gut instinct steers you in the right direction more often than not. This isn't an innate skill or a magical power, it's the result of making a conscious effort to learn at every opportunity. The exciting thing about lactation work is that every dyad does end up teaching you something new and adding to your well of insight and improves your quality of care.

Your ability to think critically may be impaired by your biases or your own personal history. If you had difficulty breastfeeding your own baby, you may be triggered by your clients' experiences. Members of a dominant culture will need to work through the way their privilege may be influencing the way they provide care. Self-awareness and a willingness to change will help you mitigate the impact of your limitations.

There is a wide range of compliance in the families we work with. Some parents will take your recommendations to heart, make them their own, and pursue their goals wholeheartedly. Others will implement absolutely nothing in the care plan and come back to you asking why they are still having issues. This can be extremely frustrating, and when this happens, remember that it's their life, not yours. The goal is to empower our clients to meet their personal goals, not to impose upon them our ideas of the "right" way to do things.

Questions for self-reflection:

- Do I recognize the importance of treating each family individually?
- Am I willing to push my comfort levels with uncertainty and complexity?
- Do I see the value in avoiding a rush to judgement or a quick fix?

- Will I seek out continuing education above and beyond what is required, and am I willing to change my practices when I learn something new? Will I continue to do so?
- Do I value constructive criticism?

Recommended resources:

- Supporting Sucking Skills in Breastfeeding Infants by Catherine Watson Genna
- Selecting and Using Breastfeeding Tools by Catherine Watson Genna
- The Breastfeeding Mother's Guide to Making More Milk by Diana West
- Finding Sufficiency: Breastfeeding with Insufficient Glandular Tissue by Diana Cassar-Uhl
- Sweet Sleep: Nighttime and Naptime Strategies for the Breastfeeding Family by Diane Wiessinger, Diana West, Linda J. Smith, and Teresa Pitman
- Impact of Birthing Practices on Breastfeeding by Linda J. Smith
- GOLD Lactation
- iLactation
- Academy of Breastfeeding Medicine Blog

History Taking and Documentation

"Chart or it didn't happen." This truism from the nursing world means that every aspect of an encounter with our clients must be written down in a legible, coherent, and objective fashion. If you take insurance, you know that your client charts may be requested by the insurance provider in order to see if the services provided match the coding assigned to the chart. Your client has the right to request their chart at any time. And if you are seeing a client multiple times or provide phone or email follow up, good charting is necessary to refresh your memory so that each client encounter builds effectively on the encounter that came before.

Taking an effective history and creating a comprehensive chart for your client involves some writing skills, but there are many charting solutions (both paper and paperless) that use checkboxes and templates in order to simplify the process. You do not need to be computer savvy, and can certainly do all of your charting and care plan creation on paper. There are even templates for sending a report to the pediatrician, which can be sent by regular mail, therefore keeping technology out of the entire process.

There are limitations to templated charting, which you will discover once you are actively seeing clients. You will want to add commentary when a situation doesn't exactly fit the norm, and you will want to tailor recommendations to make them appropriate for your client's specific situation. This is where private practice differs from hospital practice—you are not limited by a set of predetermined rules, actions, or procedures. However you structure your history taking and documentation processes, you will need to be thorough and clear as these are medical records that may be requested by the client or an appropriate third party.

Ultimately, you will need a documentation and charting solution that both saves you time and allows you the flexibility you need to offer individualized care. If you offer home visits, this system will need to be portable, and you will need to have a place where you can securely lock your files. You are not required to have a computer or tablet, but if you use any technology in your practice, your use of it must be compliant with HIPAA regulations.

Questions for self-reflection:

- Am I motivated to learn how to keep accurate and comprehensive charts for my clients, even when it gets tedious?

- Do I have a place in my home where I can store a locked box or filing cabinet with client files?
- Am I willing to apply what I learn about HIPAA to my practices, even when it is inconvenient to do so?

Recommended resources:

- History and Assessment: It's All in the Details by Denise Altman
- Paperless Private Practice for the IBCLC by Annie Frisbie
- Legal and Ethical Issues for the IBCLC by Elizabeth C. Brooks

Communications Skills

Effective communications skills are not only integral to the IBCLC, but fundamental. How you present information is just as important as important as the information itself. Because we do not diagnose or prescribe, but rather assess and recommend, our job is to teach our clients to self-manage their situations and adopt preventive behaviors. You can be as right as the day is long, but if your client does not understand you, they will not be able to follow through with your recommendations.

Effective communications incorporates these crucial elements:

- Correct information
- Up-to-date recommendations
- Empathy and responsiveness
- Written and verbal proficiency
- Cultural competency
- Inclusive language
- Protection of client privacy
- Interpretation and use of nonverbal cues

Our clients need us to meet them where they are, and that means putting them first in our communications with them. Empathy, where we validate their feelings, builds trust; whereas sympathy, where we judge their feelings, makes the encounter all about us. Using inclusive language shows that we will not be making assumptions, which allows clients the space to be truthful with us.

But before we can speak, we first need to listen. Allow your clients to tell their stories without interruption, judgment, or commentary. Many times we will find ourselves working with a parent who has experienced birth trauma, who may have felt ignored, disregarded, or even violated. Families also need a way to express the pain, anger, and/or frustration they feel because breastfeeding isn't going well. Through active listening, we show them that we are engaged and present with them, and we send a powerful message that their feelings matter—that they matter.

Questions for self-reflection:

- Am I willing to take extra time in crafting professional written responses to my clients, instead of writing the way I might write to a friend or family member?
- Do I see the value in meeting clients where they are, and removing my personal biases from my communications with my clients?
- Do I recognize that my own history with birth or breastfeeding (or lack thereof) may influence the way I practice, and am I willing to work on my personal triggers in order to keep the focus on my clients?
- If I am the member of a dominant group, am I willing to explore my privilege and learn how my privilege affects my communications? Am I willing to change the way I speak and write in response to what I learn about my privilege?

Recommended resources:

On active listening and empathetic communication:

- The 4 Attributes of a Good Listener
- Become a Better Listener: Active Listening
- 10 Steps To Effective Listening
- How to Be Empathetic
- Impact of Communication in Healthcare
- Nonviolent Communication: A Language of Life by Marshall B. Rosenberg
- Creating Connection: Communication Skills for Lactation Educators

On inequities in lactation and maternal healthcare:

- The Big Letdown: How Medicine, Big Business, and Feminism Undermine Breastfeeding by Kimberly Seals Allers
- Ally, Accomplice, or Simply Annoying? Resources for White Folks to Understand and Dismantle Racism by Elizabeth Brooks
- Why America's Black Mothers and Babies Are in a Life-or-Death Crisis

On interrogating privilege:

- 10 Ways to Check Your Privilege Around Poor and Working-Class Friends
- White Privilege: Unpacking the Invisible Knapsack
- Your Privilege Is Trending: Confronting Whiteness on Social Media

On birth trauma and perinatal mood disorders:

- <u>The Hidden Feelings of Motherhood by Kathleen Kendall-Tackett</u>
- <u>Understanding Birth Trauma and Its Effects on Women</u>
- <u>I can't forget the horror of my son's birth</u>
- <u>Seleni Institute Online Training</u>

Case Management

The final type of clinical skill you will need to develop is the ability to manage a client's case from initial contact, when you schedule the visit, through their "graduation." In some cases, this may mean more than one in-person visit, but often this means following up with your clients to determine if the care plan is effective. Case management also includes coordination of care with other medical professionals and support persons.

In the medical world, insurance and HIPAA run the show, which means very few of us enjoy a relationship with our primary care physician that resembles the one our parents or grandparents had with their country doctor. These structures erect financial and legal barriers that inhibit us from expecting medical professionals to be available to us "on-demand."

Because the IBCLC credential emerged out of a La Leche League, a mother-to-mother volunteer breastfeeding organization, and because the medical profession and Western culture deems breastfeeding a choice instead of a human right, our clients tend to need and expect us to be available to them. Many of them treat us more like a trusted family member or personal coach. Often insurance will only reimburse for one visit (if that), but rarely is one visit enough to sort out the kinds of complicated breastfeeding issues that private practice IBCLCs see.

We know that our clients may not get support in meeting their goals from their doctors and in the workplace, and we see the challenges they will face in advocating for themselves and their babies. For this reason, many of us are drawn to extend ourselves beyond the paid services we perform. The satisfaction that comes from walking with a family on a journey that ends in empowerment and self-efficacy cannot be underestimated.

Private practice, therefore, is work that might bleed into your personal time. You may not be able to limit your care and availability to office hours or set appointment times. It is very easy to experience slippage, where you allow client care to intrude to the point where you feel resentment. For example, postpartum anxiety may manifest itself with excessive communication. The client will text you the same questions or concerns repeatedly, and will seem to ignore the information or recommendations you are providing. Their worries may be presented with urgency, and trigger your desire to help them, and before you know it you are sucked into a text vortex that seems like it will never end.

Creating effective limits and boundaries for yourself is essential to preventing burnout, and in private practice you are the one who must establish your terms and hold yourself to them. You decide when you will engage with a client by text, and when you will slow things down with a phone call or email. You decide if you will charge for text, phone, or email follow-up (and you make sure that your clients give consent for any communication that is not by phone). You decide how much of your time you can give to your private practice, and how far you are willing to extend yourself. You set the rules, but you also get to decide when to break them. This level of freedom can be intimidating—or exhilarating.

If you spend any amount of time in private practice, inevitably you will have a client who is not happy with you. This can apply in any setting, of course, but in private practice it can be really painful when a client expresses criticism—especially when it takes the form of a post or comment on social media, or a negative online review. Resilience and humility can prove to be essential survival skills when managing the emotional ups and downs you'll face working with families during a very vulnerable time.

Questions for self-reflection:

- How do I feel about the prospect of working alone in a solo practice?
- What strategies will I need develop in order to create healthy limits and boundaries with my clients?
- Am I passionate about breastfeeding and breastfeeding support?
- If my clients are unable to achieve "perfect" breastfeeding, am I willing to work within their circumstances to help them achieve self-efficacy in managing their bodies and their babies?
- Am I willing to expose myself to criticism and negative feedback, and am I willing to see these as an opportunity for growth?

Recommended resources:

- What Is Patient-Centered Care?
- The Values and Value of Patient-Centered Care
- The 5 worst things about being an IBCLC by Rachel O'Brien
- Words from the Wise: Do's & Don'ts of Running a Private Lactation Practice by Brandy Walters
- Perspectives in Lactation: Is Private Practice for Me? By Kathy Parkes

Business Skills

As an IBCLC in private practice, you are more than just a healthcare provider—you are also running a business. Some of the hats you will wear include:

- Accountant
- Office manager
- Tech support
- Marketing
- Customer service
- Project manager
- Transportation coordinator

Expect to spend a few hours each month on behind-the-scenes tasks necessary to running your private practice. You will not be getting paid for them directly, but the fees you charge your clients should account for the work you will need to do outside of client visits. On average, a two-hour visit ends up taking about more like three to four hours of your time, when travel and administrative and billing tasks are taken into account. And that doesn't even include any follow-up you provide to them.

It also may take some time for your business to ramp up. In your first year as an IBCLC in private practice you may not be as busy as you would like to be, and you will also incur startup costs. Anticipating more expenses/less income in the first year will set your expectations appropriately. More on setting your fees in a later section.

Questions for self-reflection:

- How do I feel about taking responsibility for administrative tasks?
- Will I be able to allow time each month to run my business?
- How will I prepare for the initial costs of opening a private practice?
- What is my personal comfort level with risk and uncertainty?

Recommended resources:

- Advanced Clinical & Business Skills for Lactation Consultants in Private Practice Lecture Pack
- Birthing my practice: My first nine months as a self-employed IBCLC
- What I Wish I'd Known Before Starting a Private Practice
- 3 Common Mistakes New Private Practices Make

On obtaining small-business funding:

- Tips for Finding Small Business Grants in Canada
- Business grants and financing: Government of Canada
- U.S. Small Business Administration
- Small-Business Grants for Women: 10 Go-To Spots
- 13 Places to Find Small-Business Grants for 2017 and 2018
- The Best Grants for Your Small Business

SETTING UP YOUR IBCLC PRIVATE PRACTICE

Now that you're ready to put yourself out there as a private practice IBCLC, first you'll need to figure out who you're planning to be, how your business will work, and what you need to do to shout it to the world.

HIPAA Overview

Throughout this section of the book, I will be addressing the Health Insurance Portability and Accountability Act (HIPAA), which governs the ways in which healthcare providers and entities may manage and communicate client information using electronic technology. HIPAA is stringent and restrictive and designed to place limits on the use of technology because the kinds of information that medical professionals have access to is quite valuable.

The essence of HIPAA is simple. You can't share anything about your clients in any electronic form unless certain provisions are in place to assure HIPAA security. Sharing Protected Health Information (PHI) in an unsecured manner is called a breach, and covered entities may be subject to fines or other sanctions if they fail to protect PHI. A name is PHI; so is an appointment time. If you're communicating exclusively by phone (not text) and charting on paper, then your risk of a HIPAA violation is slim-to-none.

If you choose to incorporate email, text, cloud-based storage, or any other technology into your practice, then you need to make sure you only share or store PHI on networks that provide you with a Business Associates Agreement (BAA). This is a contractual agreement put in place between a HIPAA covered entity (i.e. you) and a person or company contracted to provide services to the HIPAA covered entity. The BAA contains assurances that the contracted company or person will protect PHI and assist the covered entity in maintaining HIPAA compliance.

If you work with any subcontractors or other professionals, such as a biller, an accountant, a scheduler, or a virtual assistant, it is recommended that you have them sign a BAA with you. Your spouse may not sign a BAA with you unless they are performing services for your private practice. This means you may not share PHI with your spouse. In the section on legal forms, I talk more about these implications for informed consent.

Even if you implement solutions that advertise themselves as "HIPAA-compliant," it is still possible to implement them in a non-compliant manner. You are the one who must comply with the law—not your devices, not your apps, not your service providers—you and you alone are responsible to meet your obligations under HIPAA. Please check out my book *Paperless Private Practice for Lactation Consultants* for a thorough explanation of how to incorporate technology into your private practice in a HIPAA-secure way.

- Paperless Private Practice for the IBCLC
- Summary of the HIPAA Security Rule
- Five Steps to Meet HIPAA Obligations and Privacy & Security Compliance
- What is the HITECH Act?
- Are You a Covered Entity?
- Am I a HIPAA Covered Entity? How Much Does It Matter If I Am Or Not? (2016 Update)
- Does the HIPAA Privacy Rule permit a doctor, laboratory, or other healthcare provider to share patient health information for treatment purposes by fax, e-mail, or over the phone?
- The Use of Technology and HIPAA Compliance
- HIPAA Compliance Checklist

Vision

Being able to create your own job description is one of the most appealing—and intimidating—features of private practice. Nobody is going to tell you what to do or how to do it. You get to be your own boss and run the show. In this section, I will help you brainstorm your ideal private practice.

Practice Setting

Your practice setting simply refers to the place where you see clients. As a private practice IBCLC, you have two options:

- Home
- Office

Let's break each of these down.

Home Visits

When you do a home visit, you are traveling to your client, either to their permanent home or a temporary place of residence. For example, in some cultures it is traditional for the new mother and the baby to live with parents or in-laws during a confinement period. You are bringing your practice to them and working with them in their space and on their terms.

Advantages:

It is tremendously convenient for parents to have us come to them. They do not even need to change out of pajamas unless they want to. And it's convenient for us, too, because we can teach them how to breastfeed in their bed, in their favorite chair, on that comfy sectional sofa with chaise extension, or even on the floor while their older toddler plays nearby.

A home visit may feel safer for a family from a non-majority culture or who do not identify along traditionally recognized gender norms. Entering a client's home gives them power that they may not have access to if they were coming to an office or clinic. This act of empowerment may increase their receptivity and inspire more feelings of self-efficacy.

I like being in client's homes because I can get such a good picture of what's going on simply through visual observation. When I wash my hands in their kitchen, I can notice if there are bottles or pump parts drying next to the sink. I can see if the pump is out on the counter or on a side table next to the couch. I get to meet other people in the life of my clients, not just their intimate partners but extended family members, other children, friends, nannies, birth and postpartum doulas, baby "nurses," and even pets. I love looking at their bookshelves and wall art and knickknacks to get a sense of everyone's personality.

When working with a family where breastfeeding is not going well (or not happening at all), coming to their home is a powerful reminder to me that I am meeting them where they are. When a difficult situation turns around, seeing clients relax while breastfeeding in their own homes is one of my favorite parts of this job, because it's a moment when I get to see them take that next step into the long marathon of parenthood. It can be a moment of sweet surrender for everyone.

Finally, if you are in the US, you may be able to deduct your mileage for driving to home visits on your taxes. Check your country, state, or province's tax codes or consult with an accountant.

Challenges:

For many, travel time is a significant barrier to providing in-home services. Here in New York City, it can take me over an hour to travel seven miles when I'm going from Queens to Brooklyn—and it's a hard seven miles of bumper-to-bumper traffic. Once I'm there, I am usually spending ten to fifteen more minutes looking for parking, and often I have to pay. My colleagues in Manhattan don't use cars at all, but carry their heavy scales and equipment suitcases on public transportation.

In less population-dense areas, you may end up covering a wider geographical area, but invariably you will run into this issue: you drove forty-five minutes to see someone in Town A, and then you get a call from someone in Town B, well within your geographic radius but on the opposite end, and now you're going to have to drive one and a half hours to your next visit. Or you'll have to say no because your babysitter has to leave right at 6 p.m. and there are just not enough hours in the day to fit this person in.

I find scheduling home visits ends up being like one of those puzzles where there are eight tiles and one open space in a three-by-three frame and you are supposed to slide the pieces one at a time until they end up in order. Every few weeks I promise myself that I am done trying to squeeze people in, that I am done trying to find extra childcare when I get an inquiry that tugs at my heartstrings, that I am done trying to move any appointment times once they are set even if it would make sense to do so. However, as soon as client calls slow down even a tiny bit, I start feeling the pressure to say yes even if it puts a strain on my schedule. Since my hours are what I want them to be, I have to remember to be a good boss to myself and give myself time off on a regular basis.

And then one of my kids will get sick, or there will be a blizzard that makes driving impossible, or my babysitter will cancel, or a client will ask to reschedule and now it's time to play home visit shuffle again. Of course, you can have scheduling mishaps and challenges in an office setting, but the travel piece is what adds the layer of complexity that can be so stressful and mentally time-consuming.

A second challenge of home visits is the flip side of one of the advantages: going inside someone else's space. You are giving up a certain level of control and this does add a certain layer of stress to the encounter. Here's a sampling of inconveniences or stressors you may encounter in your clients' homes:

Pets. I am not really an animal person (don't judge!)—I like animals and there are even some dogs and cats in my life that I have loved, but I don't enjoy being around house pets for their own sake. Also, they make me sneeze even if I have a Claritin. Some dogs will become aggressive towards strangers when there's a new baby around. But it wasn't until the littlest Yorkie you have ever seen locked me and a client in the hallway of her building—with the baby still inside the apartment—that I started telling clients up front that all animals should be secured in another room during the visit. The baby was asleep on a safe surface and the client's husband got home with the keys within forty-five minutes; we did the intake in the hallway, a first (and preferably last) for me.

Cleanliness. You will encounter a wide range when it comes to the condition of your clients' homes. In some cases, it seems like they did a full professional clean right before I showed up; in other cases, the environment may raise some red flags for basic hygiene and food safety. Either extreme may be a warning sign for a perinatal mood disorder, requiring counseling skills to address in a way that isn't judgmental. Provide consistent education on how to clean pump parts and bottles, how to safely store human milk, and safe preparation of infant formula (when necessary) regardless of your interpretation of the state of their home. Making this information part of every encounter can help prevent bias in favor of tidy clients. If you are wondering whether or not the condition of the home you are visiting falls into the realm of neglect, you will find yourself in a difficult situation (unless you are already a mandatory reporter). Chart what you see, send it in the pediatrician's report, and make sure the client gets a copy of everything so that you are not going behind their back. Then follow up with a phone call and speak directly to the pediatrician about your concerns.

Safety. This is a very real consideration when performing home visits. Never go to anyone's home unless you have had a substantial conversation with the family to establish the existence of a pregnant person or a lactating person and a baby, and make sure someone knows where you are (more on how to do that in the upcoming section on informed consent). Take precautions when parking your car—but please don't write off a potential client just because of where they live. Concerns over a neighborhood may say more about your biases than your safety. Depending on where you live, you may want to specify that any firearms in the home be locked up for the duration of your visit. If you are alarmed by anything you see to the point where you feel that the baby or any older children are in immediate danger, you may need to call the appropriate agency in your state, or even 911.

Cultural and religious practices and/or family preferences. Your client may need or want you to behave in a certain way when you are in their home. For example, some cultures (and most people in New York City) want you to take off your shoes when you enter their home. Some families may offer you something to eat or drink, and it may be hard to tell if they are just being polite or if they are from a cultural tradition where feeding guests is an important value. I usually say yes to a glass of water (no ice) and make a comment about how I always forget to drink enough water (true). If it's early in the morning and I'm offered coffee by the client's partner or family member, and they have a look on their face like they are really into coffee, and I didn't bring my own coffee with me, I will say yes. That is how I ended up drinking the best coffee I have ever had in the home of a very sweet Palestinian family (and let me tell you I was very productive and energetic for the rest of the day). The flip side is that I have food allergies, so sometimes clients will offer me cookies and I have to say no. Even though people are generally understanding, it's still a little bit of a weird moment. In the non-food realm, some families will not share the baby's name until after a naming ceremony. I recommend asking clients in advance, "Please tell me about any cultural or religious practices that may impact our time together." As I tell my own children, use good manners and things will generally turn out all right.

Home decor that may provoke negative emotions. Your clients' homes reflect their personal values, and those may differ from your own. You may see signage for a political candidate you loathe, you may see books on topics with which you disagree, and you may see signs of values that are opposite to your own. All families deserve your best whether or not your life choices are compatible. If you will find it difficult to mask your personal feelings when confronted with lifestyles that are different to your own, then home visits may not be the right setting for you.

The television is on or music is playing. Everyone has a different threshold for tolerating ambient background noise. I can generally tune it out and will only ask to turn it off if it is distracting to the baby. Sometimes I have been in a small apartment where a sports game is on and family members are actively involved in watching. This can be a tricky dynamic and you may not feel like you can ask them to turn it down or off. Recognizing that breastfeeding is happening in a home that might be noisy is part of meeting a family where they are, and you can incorporate education on how babies can be distracted by noise and light into your visit, as well as information on AAP recommendations for babies and screens.

Other children. I had a visit once where an adorable 3-year-old kept interrupting me because he wanted the "doctor" to play with him. I like children generally, so I have a lot of patience, but that doesn't mean it isn't challenging to work around a toddler or preschooler.

The final challenge of home visits is what to do with all your stuff. Every time you go on a home visit you are bringing your scale, various tools, any handouts or educational materials you like to give to families, and your charting device or paperwork. On more than one occasion I have left my scale at home because I simply forgot I had taken it out of the trunk of my car overnight due to extreme cold or heat.

- <u>My Home Visit Supply Kit</u>

- Safety Tips for Home Visits From a Veteran NYC Social Worker
- Safety Tips for Home Healthcare Workers
- Home Health Care Patients and Safety Hazards in the Home: Preliminary Findings
- Topic Number 510 - Business Use of Car

Office Visits

As an IBCLC providing in-office visits, you have your own space and clients come to you for visits. Some IBCLCs share space with other IBCLCs or other medical professionals, or have a group practice.

Advantages:

You will have more control over your schedule if you work out of an office. Because you don't have to account for travel time, you can stack clients one after the other with only a short break between, meaning you can possibly see more clients in a day. For example, in an eight-hour day, you can fit in four ninety-minute home visits, allowing for thirty minutes of travel for each one—and you'll be eating lunch in your car. In an office setting, in eight hours you can schedule five ninety-minute sessions with clients, allow for fifteen minutes between each client, and take a thirty-minute lunch break.

Seeing more clients in a day may also mean charging less per client than if you are doing home visits, and that may incentivize clients to book follow-up visits, enabling you to track progress and outcomes.

If you have an office, you can leave all of your equipment and supplies in one place. You will have more room to stock items for rent or sale, such as hospital-grade pumps and parts, at-breast supplementers, and nipple shields. A locked filing cabinet can store all of your files and charts, and you can have a bookshelf with all of your textbooks and references available at all times.

For accounting/tax purposes, you will have a separate office location and many of these expenses may be deductible. This office can be in your home if it is a separate space. Tax laws are subject to change and you must always check the applicable laws and tax codes for your country, province, and/or state.

Challenges:

If you do not have a room in your home that can serve as an office, you may end up needing to pay rent for your space, whether or not your practice is in a busy season or a slow season. You will need to purchase furnishings for your space, and you will need to keep it very clean. Your county, town, or neighborhood covenant may have legal provisions you will need to comply with if you are setting up a home office. When sharing a space or hiring staff, you will need to be conscious of HIPAA; for example, if you set up a WiFi network or server it will be important to include security features.

Seeing clients in an office setting means that you will not get a sense of what their home life is like outside of their own descriptions. Parent and baby may not be as relaxed as they might be in their own home, and they may have difficulty replicating positions if they don't have a chair like the one in your office.

- Things To Consider When Working From Home
- Home Office: When The Therapy Office Is At Home
- Protecting Personal Information: A Guide for Business
- HIPAA for Smaller Providers and Businesses
- Home Office Deduction

Additional Services Offered

In addition to the management and care of a breastfeeding family, you may want to offer other services to your community.

Classes, Support Groups, and Clinics

Classes, support groups, and clinics offer ways for you to use your clinical skills to reach groups of people, and each one has a slightly different flavor to it. Running sessions like these requires a blend of public speaking, crowd control, content development, and strategic thinking. As I've mentioned before, often none of these are innate abilities that you either have or don't have, but qualities that can be developed and strengthened if you're motivated.

If you have space in your home and relatively little overhead, these offerings can be an easy way to market your services and style to new clients and provide ongoing support to current clients. When you have to pay to rent a space, your class, support group, or clinic may end up being a loss leader, where you spend more money than you make but still receive the publicity benefits. Shadowing another IBCLC with an established group can be a great way to discern whether or not group work is for you.

Before you can dream up your perfect group offering, if you don't have room in your own home, you'll need to find a space. Expect to pay something for your space, so rule out any options that are going to charge so much that you won't have anything left for yourself—or worse, go out of pocket. Some IBCLCs in my area have agreements where the space takes a certain percentage of the attendance, and this can work very well when partnering with a space that is also connected with the birthing/postpartum world. Ideas include:

- Doctor's offices—specifically pediatricians, midwives, chiropractors, or preferred frenotomy providers
- Freestanding birth centers
- Yoga studios
- Health and wellness centers like the YMCA
- Libraries
- Places of worship

- Coworking spaces
- Community centers
- Schools
- Doula collectives with a physical space

Chapter 2 of Elizabeth Brooks's book Legal and Ethical Issues for the IBCLC will help you better understand the IBCLC-client relationship because those concepts are applicable to a group setting, too. Brooks is a frequent poster/commenter in IBCLC groups on Facebook and often speaks to issues related to providing support or clinical care in a group setting.

- Legal and Ethical Issues for the IBCLC by Elizabeth Brooks
- Developing and Sustaining Breastfeeding Peer-Support Programs

Classes

Classes use a standardized curriculum to provide education on a specific topic with no access to any direct clinical management. These classes can be intimate—possibly for even just one family— or large—presenting at grand rounds at your local hospital or speaking at a baby fair or parenting conference. Common topics for classes include:

- Prenatal preparation for breastfeeding/chestfeeding
- Back-to-work counseling
- Initiating induced lactation and adoptive breastfeeding/chestfeeding
- Breastfeeding past infancy and tandem nursing
- Case studies

Teaching a class requires curriculum development and advanced preparation. Familiarity with hospital culture can be very helpful when teaching prenatal classes, as ideal initiation may not be possible even with an unmedicated vaginal birth. You may want to learn how to create presentations in PowerPoint or Keynote. Developing handouts customized with your contact information is a great way to help class members book a home or office visit, or to leverage presentation attendees into referral sources.

Classes don't have to be in person, either. Many consultants in all industries are creating webinars (recorded or live), using podcast technology, and developing apps to disseminate educational materials and hopefully make some money at it. And if you've always dreamed of giving a TED Talk, consider developing your area of expertise into a lecture for other lactation professionals. Check out LactSpeak to see what's out there already so that you can carve out your own niche.

- Teaching prenatal breastfeeding classes
- Signs You Have a Good Breastfeeding Class
- Breastfeeding Classes: Essential or Outdated?
- LactSpeak

Support Groups

A support group is a focused discussion moderated by a facilitator who is usually licensed by the state or credentialed by a recognized organization. In the breastfeeding world, La Leche League is one of the more visible providers of group support, offering free meetings, but because the ideological flavor of LLL is not for everyone, there is more than enough room for other types of support groups.

Your group may be open to current clients only, as a way to offer ongoing follow-up support, or it may be open to the public, as a way to publicize your services and gain more clients. A support group is not an appropriate setting for clinical services but rather an opportunity to create a safe, supportive atmosphere where members can share their struggles and receive emotional validation and generalized strategies for coping and making progress. A good rule of thumb is to assume wellness and if there are signs of complexity or pathology requiring any kind of clinical intervention, to immediately refer out. Even if you are qualified to address the concerns, a group setting is not the place for it.

To be an effective support group facilitator, you will need to develop counseling skills specific to a group setting:

- Topic development and presentation
- Moderating the flow of conversation
- How to deal with difficult situations, such as when one person dominates the conversation, or if a group member says something offensive or inappropriate
- Keeping things vague: "many families find…" instead of "you should…"

Support groups can often work well in partnership with another parenting or perinatal organization, as part of a cornucopia of services for parents. Check out the Motherhood Center in New York City as a good example of what that might look like. Retail stores targeting new families and freestanding birth centers are also often open to hosting support groups.

- <u>4 Mental Health Benefits Of Support Groups, From Encouragement To Better Coping Skills</u>
- <u>Needed: More Support Groups for Working Moms</u>
- La Leche League
- The Motherhood Center

Clinics

By its very name, a clinic means you are offering some degree of clinical care to attenders. If the attender is your current client, you have a preexisting clinical relationship and should document the encounter in their chart (more on that coming up in the section on Typical IBCLC Client Workflow). If the attender is someone you have never met before, best practices are to have them sign an informed consent, take a history, chart the encounter, and refer out to the appropriate healthcare provider(s) for continued monitoring (and that can include referring out to yourself for an in-person consult). Once this happens, all HIPAA provisions are in place.

Clinics often have a scale to perform pre- and post-feed weights. Some who run clinics will perform oral exams to identify possible tongue tie or other oral anomalies. There is a wide range of opinion on whether or not either of these are appropriate in a clinical setting, where you may not have the time to fully explain the implications to the parent. You will need to explore your own comfort level with the skills you use in a group setting, and take care to ensure that attendees are not receiving information in a vacuum.

A clinic can also incorporate other IBCLCs or providers from other disciplines. For example, some IBCLCs will partner with an occupational therapist or bodyworker to provide post-frenotomy support for families who have been treated by a preferred provider. In a team approach, you split potential revenue from the clinic, but may be able to address needs in a more targeted way and improve health outcomes for families.

Find an IBCLC in your area with a long-running clinic and ask if you can attend as an observer to see how they manage the intricacies of providing clinical care in a group setting. Crowd-sourcing can also be a great way to learn how other IBCLCs structure their clinics. Start small, by facilitating a breastfeeding support group without a clinical component, and see where that takes you.

Equipment Rentals and Sales

Having a stock of hospital-grade pumps and calibrated baby scales may provide you with an additional source of income. Families will put down a deposit, pay you a weekly or monthly fee, and receive their deposit back once they've returned the pump or scale to you in the agreed-upon condition. You may also want to sell the kit that goes with the pump, as well as different flange sizes. You may also want to carry and potentially sell items like at-breast supplementers.

Adding these services may open you up to potential conflict of interest, where you have financial motivation to recommend a product or intervention because you stand to make a profit from it. *Legal and Ethical Issues for the IBCLC* by Elizabeth Brooks has a must-read chapter on this topic. At the same time, you may want the client to have access to the equipment at the time of the visit, rather than sending them out to a retail or store or having them wait for delivery from an online store. For direct equipment sales, the best way to avoid a conflict of interest is to charge the client your cost for the product, so that you are not making a profit. You could also consider deducting the cost of the items on your taxes and simply giving away these items.

Hospital-grade pumps and baby scales are too costly to give away. Before choosing to include rentals in your business model, consider how easy or difficult it is for families to obtain a hospital-grade pump in your area. If you live in a place where there are reputable retail stores or suppliers of durable medical equipment (DME), you can avoid the conflict of interest by providing clients with at least two options in addition to renting it from you. In your charting, make sure you are documentation the clinical indication for a hospital-grade pump.

In rural areas, access to this type of equipment may be difficult or impossible. You may think it necessary to keep a stock of hospital-grade pumps to rent to clients who may otherwise not be able to get one. But in this day and age, families always have the option to rent a pump online (and even go through their insurance for it). Providing families with those options allows them to make a freely considered choice about whether or not they want the pump that day, or if they want to go through their insurance but possibly wait to get the pump. Remember to present hand expression as an option to any of your families who need to increase supply—not only is it a good technique for any breastfeeder to master, but learning this skill increases client self-efficacy and may even eliminate the need for a hospital grade pump. You may feel that it is urgent for a client to begin pumping with a hospital-grade pump immediately, but every client deserves options and has the right to refuse any intervention presented to them. Directing your clients towards one specific course of action that you stand to profit from is at the heart of the concept of conflict of interest. There is always another path worth considering.

- <u>Ethical Issues in Breastfeeding Support</u>
- <u>Legal and Ethical Issues for the IBCLC by Elizabeth Brooks</u>
- <u>Go Milk Yourself: You Have Power. Express It! by Francie Webb</u>

Telehealth

Telehealth, or telemedicine, in which healthcare providers use telephone and internet technology to have virtual consults with clients and patients, comes with a great deal of promise and a boatload of pitfalls. You may find the idea extremely appealing, especially as a way to reach families in isolated communities without access to in-person IBCLC care. Health and Human Services, a division of the US Government, has identified telehealth as "a cost-effective alternative to the more traditional face-to-face way of providing medical care" and has been working on integrating telehealth into Medicaid.

In order to provide telehealth sessions, either as virtual follow-ups for your current clients or as a standalone service, you will need a HIPAA-compliant telehealth platform and a fast and secure internet connection. (Your HIPAA-compliant platform is useless if you're using over a free public WiFi network.) Your client will also need to have access to the same telehealth platform. You might need to pay for the platform; your client shouldn't incur any fees on their end for the tech side of things.

Insurance will generally not cover telemedicine at this time, and there are no provisions for telehealth for lactation support in the Affordable Care Act. These services will be out-of-pocket for your clients. You may find that clients are willing to pay without reimbursement in exchange for the convenience of a quick visit, or because they have no in-person option.

When offering telemedicine, all the same rules apply as to an in-person visit. You must get informed consent, you must chart the encounter, you must send a written care plan, and you must send out reports to appropriate members of the client's healthcare team.

A huge downfall of telehealth for the IBCLC is the inability to perform physical assessments or counseling strategies that require touch. You cannot perform an oral exam; you cannot palpate a plugged duct; you cannot feel the tension in a baby's body; you cannot use your hands to make modifications to positioning. Be very cautious about overstepping when using telehealth, making it clear to clients that telehealth is not a substitute for in-person medical care, and be proactive about referring out when a client needs more than just counseling.

- HIPAA Guidelines on Telemedicine
- Practitioner Pointer: Does the use of Skype raise HIPAA compliance issues?
- Free, HIPAA-Secure Online Therapy Software (2018 Update)
- HHS: Telemedicine Is Not New, But Recent Advancements Inflate Its Potential
- HHS Report Outlines Problems, Potential Of Telemedicine
- Telemedicine Could Be Great, If People Stopped Using It Like Uber
- Thin Ice Ahead: Offering Lactation Help On Social Media And Cell Phones
- Telemedicine and Medicaid

Education, Mentoring, and Professional Speaking

There are many opportunities for the private practice IBCLC outside of working directly with families in a clinical or group setting. If you enjoy teaching, coaching, writing, and/or public speaking, consider developing skills to bring training, education, and guidance to current and aspiring IBCLCs. Some ideas include:

- Speaking at conferences on the professional circuit
- Developing a webinar for an online conference or your own platform
- Creating an in-person training program that offers credits toward IBLCE certification or CERPs for recertification
- Working with interns as a mentor one-on-one or in a small group setting
- Writing a book on a topic you're passionate about

When it comes to mentoring, there is some debate within the lactation communities about how charging interns can be a barrier to entry for potential IBCLCs coming from underrepresented groups. Because IBCLCs of color are vastly underrepresented in the profession, many advocate for waiving fees to mentor interns of color in order to increase their presence in the community.

The flip side of this argument is that our field is predominantly composed of women, who are often encouraged to undervalue their worth in the marketplace. And aspirants from disadvantaged backgrounds need to be able to see a pathway to profitability within the profession itself—including the potential to charge a fair price to educate future IBCLCs.

One way to move beyond this divide is to have a frank conversation with yourself and acknowledge what privileges you are bringing to the profession. Once you are able to ascertain what you have in the privilege bank, you will be able to appropriately assess what you can—and should—give away so that our profession can include all kinds of people from all walks of life.

- <u>LactSpeak</u>
- <u>Racial Inequities in Breastfeeding: My Commitment to be a Mentor</u>

Setting Fees and Income Goals

For many, deciding what to charge is the scariest part about going into private practice. Charge too little and you'll never break even; charge too much and you'll have no clients. You need to find the sweet spot where you can make a profit after covering your expenses while staying within acceptable ranges for your community's cost of living.

If you live in an area where there are a lot of IBCLCs, you can do some research to see what others are charging and get a sense of the range out there. Consider offering to buy a local colleague coffee and ask them how they set their fees, or ask in an IBCLC networking group. Some may not want to discuss financial details, but others may be happy to share information with you.

You may think that if you are a newer IBCLC that you should charge less—after all, you're less experienced therefore not worth as much. There are several things wrong with this statement.

It is possible to set a fee so low that you literally can't afford to work for it. You are basically subsidizing a volunteer job, and nothing will lead to burnout faster than working and not getting paid. Volunteering has value that cannot be underestimated, but when you work, you should work for a fair and sustainable fee. The mushy middle may kill your business.

As an IBCLC, you have met the highest standard for credentialing in the lactation world. There are professionals out there without the IBCLC credential who are charging market rate for services; by charging less as an IBCLC you dilute the power of the credential.

If there is a community consensus about fees, that means that others have learned what they need to charge to be able to afford to work. If you charge less, you may potentially drive everyone's fees down as clients try to negotiate. By undervaluing yourself, you damage the entire community and may drive other IBCLCs out of business. Trust me, you need them—there's no advantage in cornering the market on breastfeeding help at an unsustainably low rate.

If you're still thinking, "Those other IBCLCs charge a lot of money, how can I possibly charge that much right out of the gate?" There's a very simple answer.

Charge what you are worth, and make yourself worth it.

Offer clients a two-hour visit at the market rate. That's what your credential and potential are worth. But when you are just starting out, you are going to have to work much harder than an experienced IBCLC to make your fee worth it.

You may have to stay with your clients for three hours. You may end up spending hours on the phone with them. You may have to put time into researching more about their situation. You may opt to give up your time to accompany them to a frenotomy provider or a breast specialist or an occupational therapist or even to another IBCLC with more experience. This is how you learn—by giving more for your clients' money, not by charging them less.

If you live in an area where there are few to no other IBCLCs, or if the other IBCLCs in your area are not publicly publishing their rates, you will need to come up with a living wage for yourself. You must account for your expenses, your travel time, your childcare costs (if applicable), continuing education, and the time you will spend on tasks like scheduling, billing, and client communications. After you have eliminated those expenses, determine your monthly household expenses (or your portion of your family's expenses) and set goals for paying off debts and building up savings. You may not get there right away, but knowing what you need to pay your bills and save will help you value your services appropriately.

Turn this into a monthly income goal, then set yourself a client goal that will pay that monthly income to you. Assume that an average home visits will last about two hours, will involve an hour of travel, will require thirty to sixty minutes of administrative work, and may include two to four more hours of follow-up while you are still learning the ropes of private practice. An office visit won't require travel but will still have the admin work and follow-up, and will include time spent on office maintenance. As you grow in proficiency, you will be able to maximize the time spent with your clients, and minimize the time you are spending on follow-up that is technically unpaid.

This outlook works whether you want to have a busy practice seeing clients full time, or you want to work part time because of family obligations or another job. The point is that you want to make sure that you're using your time efficiently and wisely to make room to structure a live/work balance that works for your specific situation.

Consider offering package deals, where clients can arrange multiple visits for a reduction in total fee, or a concierge service, where clients pay a premium to have access to you within a certain period of time. You can team up with another birth professional to offer bundled services. And while you may need to give phone and email and text support away for free in the first few years of your practice, once you have honed your skills you may want to consider charging this kind of follow up.

It's said that any new business takes a few years before it is profitable, and the same is likely true of private practice. Keep in mind that you are both boss and employee. As employee, it's your job to work as hard as you can for the success of your company. As boss, it's your job to create a business model that can pay your employees what they are worth.

Those of you coming from a volunteer breastfeeding support background may have a hard time transitioning to paid work. I want you to know that you are not alone, and that volunteering can still be a part of your life. Just draw clear boundaries around those two spheres, and never feel guilty for charging money for your paid work.

I'm not going to lie to you, private practice is scary. You'll have times of abundance and other times when your phone doesn't ring at all. That's why you need to keep a big-picture view of your income goals. You aren't just working to cover the babysitter you paid today, you're aiming for an annual salary that you can live on. You may not get there in your first year, but you'll never get there if you don't set your goals and value yourself appropriately from the outset.

- Seeing Yourself as a Businessperson
- A 5-Step Guide To Setting Your Freelance Rates Perfectly
- The Freelance Rates Calculator We've All Been Waiting For
- Price Fixing
- Don't Try to Grow Your Business by Undercutting the Competition

Structure

Before you begin seeing clients, you will need to structure your business so that it has everything you need to operate effectively, legally, and within your scope of practice. If you are a licensed medical professional, your scope of practice may supersede the IBCLC scope of practice, and may have additional requirements.

And if you're already an IBCLC and worried that you haven't set your practice up correctly? Don't worry—it's not too late. The ideas in this section will work for you, too.

Creating a Business Entity

I am not an accountant or an attorney, so I am not equipped to advise you in a meaningful way on how to structure the financial side of your business. However, I can provide a general overview of the landscape of corporate structures so that you can ask the right questions towards forming the entity that works for you. Think of your business entity like a hat you put on when you engage in professional activities.

The primary element you need is an Employer Identification Number (EIN), also known as a Tax ID, generated by the Internal Revenue Service (IRS). It's like the business equivalent of a social security number. You will want an EIN if you are going to have any interactions with insurance companies, either by contracting directly with them or through providing a superbill for your clients to submit for reimbursement (more on that in the section on your accounting infrastructure). At the time of writing, there is no fee to apply directly for an EIN.

You can apply for an EIN for yourself, or you can set up a corporation to create a separation between your business identity and your personal identity, and protect your assets in the event that your business faces litigation of any kind. Common corporation types include the Limited Liability Company (LLC) and the Subchapter S Corporation (S-Corp). Having a business entity allows you to open up business checking and/or savings accounts, which may have better rates than personal accounts, and can make business lines of credit available to you to help you grow your business.

Creating a corporation will cost you money, and those fees will vary by state. Forming a corporation may seem like a daunting process, but there are many online services that will take care of the paperwork for you. There may be tax advantages to running your private practice income through a corporation; however, those will vary year-to-year and state-to-state. Your corporation will need to be reported on your taxes, and you will probably want to work with an accountant.

While you can form a corporation online, I recommend working directly with an attorney to set up your business identity so that you get off to the right start. Your attorney will advise on the best structure for you based on your needs and the regulations specific to your state of residence. If you have a professional license, that may impact the type of corporation you can choose.

Small Business/Entrepreneur Resources:

- US Small Business Administration
- Online Genius Membership (Legal Forms and Training for Entrepreneurs)
- SCORE: Free and Confidential Business Advice for Entrepreneurs and Small businesses
- Do-it-yourself Legal for Online Entrepreneurs

EIN & NPI:

- How To Apply for an EIN
- Do You Need a New EIN?
- When, If Ever, Do You Get a New NPI Number and Other NPI Questions

Limited Liability and S-Corp Resources:

- To LLC or not to LLC? That is the IBCLC private practitioner's question
- What Is the Difference Between a Professional LLC & a Professional Service Corporation?
- What are the Tax Differences Between an S Corporation and an LLC?
- Should Your Business Be an LLC or an S Corp?
- I'm Starting a Counseling Practice… Do I Need an LLC?

- Should I Establish an LLC for my Income as an Occupational Therapist?
- Should You Be an LLC?
- Should an Independent Contractor Form an LLC?
- LLC or Corporation - Which Should I Select for My Business?
- The Better Choice for Entity Selection: LLC or S Corporation?
- 5 Reasons Why an LLC is the Right Structure for Your Startup
- Should You Form an LLC for Your Small Business?
- When To Form An LLC (Limited Liability Company)

Essential Elements

Whether or not you form an LLC, you will need to have certain elements in place in order for your practice to work properly. I recommend completing all of these tasks before seeing your first client in order to avoid any unforeseen bureaucratic, financial, or legal complications down the road.

License

If you live in one of the US states that currently licenses IBCLCs, then you are required to comply with fees and regulations imposed by your state licensing board before seeing clients in private practice. If your state does not currently have licensure for IBCLCs, consider getting involved with your local chapter of USLCA. Not all IBCLCs are in favor of licensure, so take time to understand what's at stake in your state so you can decide where you stand.

- Should I Care About State Licensing for IBCLCs?
- Licensure for IBCLCs FAQ

NPI

The National Provider Identifier (NPI) is a unique number assigned to you that you are required to use in all communications related to financial or administrative transactions. Under the Health Insurance Portability and Accountability Act (HIPAA), in order to communicate with any insurance provider about your clients, you will need an NPI. It is advisable to obtain an EIN before applying for your NPI. There is no fee to apply for an NPI.

This provision is not limited to in-network providers. At the time of this writing, Affordable Care Act (ACA), insurance providers are required to provide comprehensive lactation support with no cost-sharing to the member. Under the law, insurance providers are supposed to provide in-network lactation consultants, and if no in-network provider is available, members can submit for out-of-network reimbursement. This means that if you are not in-network with an insurance company, you must provide your client with proof of payment suitable for submission to their insurance company, called a superbill (more on that later).

- National Provider Identifier Standard
- Frequently Asked Questions about the NPI
- How else does the Affordable Care Act impact breastfeeding families?

Liability Insurance

When you became an IBCLC, you also became a healthcare provider, and that means opening yourself up to the risk that a client will be unhappy with the services you provide, or will not implement your care plan and have an adverse result. A liability insurance policy protects you, your business, and your personal assets in the event that a client files a lawsuit against you for malpractice. While you may have never heard of this happening to another IBCLC, and possibly can't imagine it happening to you, I urge you to consider liability insurance as a non-negotiable cost of doing business. If you live in a state with IBCLC licensure, you may be required to have liability insurance as a condition of your license. You can purchase it yourself directly or go through a registered agent.

- CM&F Group
- Nicholas Hill Group
- Proliability
- Medical Professional Liability Insurance

Legal Forms

Legal forms are a necessary component of your private practice because they define your relationship with your clients in a way that assures them that you will maintain certain standards when working with them. They also ensure certain protections for you in the event that your client is unhappy with the care you have provided. By clearly stating the parameters of your relationship, you manage client expectations and set the tone for your clinical relationship.

First and foremost, the IBLCE Code of Professional Conduct stipulates that you must obtain permission from your client in order to share their information with another member of the care team, and before taking and/or sharing any pictures or videos of the client or their baby. It's advisable to have your client sign a release prior to starting your care that grants permission to you to consult with their other care providers, and that explains your policy on pictures and videos. Under no circumstances are you permitted to take or especially share/publish pictures of your clients or their babies without express written permission. They are the owners of their faces and they control where, when, and how any images are taken, published, or shared.

Many IBCLCs also include a blanket informed consent within this release form and call the document "Consent for Care." You describe what generally happens within the context of a visit, and the client signs that they understand what may happen and give their permission for you to examine and touch them and their babies. This consent is not specifically covered in the IBLCE Code of Professional Conduct, but as informed consent is the cornerstone of all clinical care you must obtain your client's express permission before you perform any physical examination of the client or their baby. You could ask permission each time, or you could have your client sign a consent form in advance covering the physical exam of client and baby, as well as any other standard procedures you perform in the course of an IBCLC visit.

If a procedure is not covered in your informed consent, you must obtain and document consent within the course of the visit. One example might be the consent to have someone else present during the visit. A client may have indicated that her partner will be in the room for the visit, but did not mention that her mother-in-law will also be there. You must document that this client has given her consent for her mother-in-law to be present.

Your standard consent may include permission to communicate with the client's pediatrician, midwife, or OB, or with another care provider such as an oral surgeon, an ENT, or a chiropractor. You may not chat about your client using personal details with your colleagues without express permission from your client, and this could be included in your consent. I get a lot of referrals from a dear friend who is a childbirth educator, but I never tell her if I've seen one of her clients without asking for permission in advance. Your clients can tell the world that they hired you as a lactation consultant; you may tell absolutely no one that someone was your client without that client's permission. Your client may not want to grant a blanket consent for you to communicate with their care providers or colleagues, and that is their right. You would still be able to ask them on a case-by-case basis ("May I share today's care plan with your pediatrician, Dr. So-and-So?") and document if consent was given or withheld.

Communicating your payment policies may also be included in your consent form. You will want to mention specific out-of-pocket fees for the services you provide, how you work with insurance if you are in-network, cancellation and refund policies, and the extent of and limitations to any follow up care you plan to provide.

Because you have an NPI, you are considered a HIPAA-covered entity, and you must also include a Notice of Privacy Practices that informs your clients about their rights concerning any of their Protected Health Information (PHI) that is stored or shared online. You may be familiar with this notice as the form that you sign whenever you go to a new doctor for a first time, or periodically at your primary care physician's office.

As a reminder, you will need a Business Associates Agreement (BAA) with any providing services with you or for you so that you may share PHI on a limited basis. This includes all cloud-based services. For example, a free Google Calendar or Apple's iCal synced over iCloud cannot be used in a HIPAA-compliant way. For more information on integrating cloud-based systems, please see my other book *Paperless Private Practice for Lactation Consultants.*

Your spouse or partner or primary support person does not count as a Business Associate unless they have been hired by you to perform services for your private practice. However, there may be situations where you need to share a PHI on a limited basis, and you can ask your clients to grant consent for those situations. For example, because I do home visits, I want someone else to know where I am at all times in case something happens and I do not come home. My consent for care form expressly states the name of the person I will be sharing my client's address with, and also indicates that I will be using GPS technology to navigate to their home.

When communicating with your clients online, best practices are to use a secure messaging platform (more in the section on communications). If you believe your clients will be sending you texts and emails even if you ask them not to (and this happens all the time), you may want to consider including that in your consent for care as well.

As always, whenever you are creating anything that someone else will sign, you should consult with your own legal counsel. I also strongly urge all IBCLCs to own (and read) a copy of *Legal and Ethical Issues for the IBCLC* by Elizabeth Brooks, an attorney and IBCLC. I have created a consent for care form that addresses the topics listed above and it is for sale in my store. The Department of Health and Human Services has created a free Model Notice of Privacy Practices that you can customize and use within your own practice.

- Legal and Ethical Issues for the IBCLC by Elizabeth Brooks
- To Whom Does the Privacy Rule Apply and Whom Will It Affect?
- Covered Entities and Business Associates
- Informed Consent
- Informed Consent for Clinical Treatment
- Model Notice of Privacy Practices (HHS)

Infrastructure

Just like a country needs roads, a water system, and a power grid in order for its citizens to thrive, your private practice needs a framework in order to be successful. Without this infrastructure, your practice will be unwieldy, unproductive, and ultimately unfulfilling.

Accounting Infrastructure

When you enter the world of private practice, you are also entering the world of self-employment, which means that you are paid directly for the work you do and no taxes are taken out by an employer. You get all of your money up front and you then have to pay taxes on that income, either at the time you file your taxes, or in the form of estimated tax payments throughout the year.

First, you need to get paid. There are two ways that IBCLCs are paid: fee for service, and through in-network contracts with insurance providers. I am not an accountant, a medical biller, or an attorney. The information provided here is gleaned from my own research and experience, and from in-person and online continuing education I've taken. It is no substitute for your own professional counsel.

Fee for Service

With fee for service, your clients are paying you at the time of the visit. You have communicated your fees up front, they have agreed to pay, and you provide them with proof of payment. You can accept payments from clients in the form of cash, check, or credit card, and you must report all income to the Internal Revenue Service (IRS) regardless of the method of payment. You are also obligated to provide your clients with a superbill, which is a receipt indicating proof of payment suitable for submitting to their insurance company for any reimbursement they are eligible for under the Affordable Care Act (ACA).

There are several components to your fees that you will want to establish up front and communicate to your clients:

- Cost of the service
- Where the services will take place
- How long the appointment will last
- What payment methods you accept
- When you expect them to pay
- What follow-up is included in your fee

Be very clear on your follow-up policies. If you offer unlimited follow-up, be prepared to come through when your clients ask you questions months later or text you fifty times in an hour. If you place limits on your follow-up, define those limits precisely so that if clients try to ask for more, you can direct them back to your payment policies.

You can set different fees for home visits or office visits, and you can set different fees for initial visits or follow-up visits. You can give discounts to clients coming to you with their next baby, or to clients who work with a doula you like or a childbirth educator you prefer. You can offer discounts based on need. You can assess a travel fee for home visits outside your regular service area, or a surcharge to see clients at night or on weekends. These additional charges are not eligible for insurance reimbursement and must be applied consistently and documented in your policies and procedures manual (more on that in another section).

However, you may NOT charge different fees for different people. Your fees must always be the same, and your policies must be consistent. For example, you can't see a client's address and charge them more because they live in a wealthy neighborhood. You can, however, offer a client a discount if they are enrolled in WIC or on Medicaid, but you are still charging them the same fee. You are free to waive your fees or surcharges or any portion thereof at your discretion, but that means that you are charging the client but not collecting full payment. In other words, if you say to a client, "My fee is $10 but I will give you a 20 percent discount," your invoice will state that you *charged* $10, but the client *paid* $8.

You may not enter into an agreement with another care provider to refer to them for a fee (or vice versa). This is a kickback, and it is illegal.

Finally, while you can raise your rates in response to market demand, you should not spike your fee to take advantage of someone who is having a hard time finding an IBCLC. Say a client writes to you and says, "I hope you can come see me, it seems like everyone I've reached out to is busy. I'd do anything to have someone come today or tomorrow." You are either available at your current rate or you're not. You must not see dollar signs in her desperation and quote her a higher fee just because you think she will pay—unless it's a surcharge that is applied consistently across all of your clients.

IBCLC fees:

- Breaking down the price of IBCLC home visits
- Are Lactation Consultants Too Pricey?

Setting fees:

- 10 Myths Therapists Believe About Setting Fees
- Setting your fees in private practice
- Setting Rates and Knowing What To Charge

Offering discounts:

- Prompt pay, cash discounts, dual fees legal for healthcare providers
- Should physicians, chiropractors, and other healthcare practitioners worry when they offer coupons for discounts to patients?
- Offer a financial break: Six ways psychologists can help patients who can no longer afford therapy.
- Should You Offer a Sliding Scale?
- How To Ethically Create And Use A Sliding Fee Scale

Insurance fraud and kickbacks:

- 10 popular healthcare provider fraud schemes (on kickbacks)
- Kickbacks are Illegal ... So What is a Kickback... It's More Than You Think!
- Kickbacks, Fee-Splitting, Corporate Practice of Medicine, Stark, MSOs: Guiding Healthcare Ventures through the Maze
- Health Care Fraud

- <u>What Is Balance Billing?</u>

Payment Processing

In order for clients to be able to use their credit cards, you must have an account with a credit card processor. One popular processor is SquareUp, and at the time of this writing it is the only one that will sign a Business Associate Agreement (BAA) with you in order to insure HIPAA compliance. With SquareUp, if you select Medical Practitioner or Medical Services as your business type, you will be able to accept cards for Flexible Spending Accounts (FSA) and Health Savings Accounts (HSA). These are special accounts where money is set aside either by the client or their employer and can only be used for healthcare expenses. Near the end of the year some clients may have FSA funds that will not roll over to the next year, so the ability to accept this type of payment may turn out to be a popular option. SquareUp charges you a fee per transaction taken out of the total payment received; your client does not pay this fee. You cannot add a surcharge to cover this fee, so take it into account when you are setting your rates.

Please note that while the BAA that SquareUp will give you does cover HIPAA compliance in the way they process and store your clients' Protected Health Information (PHI), if your client enters in their email address or phone number for a digital receipt, SquareUp will store that association and the next time your client swipes their card at a Square reader, that vendor will obtain their email address or phone number from Square. Advising your clients to opt out of digital receipts will protect you from knowingly participating in a potential HIPAA breach. You will be providing them with a superbill (more on that in a moment) as proof of payment so the SquareUp receipt may be redundant and unnecessary.

If your clients ask to pay you with another form of electronic payment, before accepting payment find out two things:

- If the payment processor protects confidentiality in a HIPAA-compliant way
- If the payment processor is meant for business transactions

You and your clients may be hit with hidden fees if you process a business transaction using a payment processor designed exclusively for person-to-person transactions. Additionally, some of these processors incorporate social aspects that can potentially expose PHI publicly. These methods are not recommended.

- Ethics of Disclosure to Clients Who Pay With Plastic or Online Transfers
- HIPAA and Credit Cards
- Banks and HIPAA: Checks & Credit Cards vs. Receipts & Invoices
- 4 Rules When Accepting Credit Card Payments to Ensure HIPAA Compliance
- Use Square, Be HIPAA Compliant! Ethics, HIPAA... and What About PayPal?
- Is Square HIPAA Compliant? How About PCI Compliant?
- PayPal for Therapists
- 4 Rules When Accepting Credit Card Payments to Ensure HIPAA Compliance

The Superbill

The IBLCE Code of Professional Conduct does not specifically state that we must provide our client with a receipt for payment. This is because IBLCE is an international organization and every country will have different laws governing healthcare. In the United States, at the time of writing we have the Affordable Care Act, which mandates that insurance providers cover lactation services without any cost-sharing to members. Certain restrictions may apply, including the right of insurance providers to restrict coverage to in-network providers.

If you have been doing this for any amount of time, you know that our clients face significant barriers in obtaining reimbursement. This coding section is meant to help you give your clients what they need, but there is never any guarantee that any of this will work once or consistently.

When your clients pay you at the time of service, in order for them to apply for reimbursement they will need a superbill, which is a special invoice containing the following information:

- Client's demographic information (name, address, birthdate)
- Client's insurance information
- Your provider information (name, address, EIN, NPI)
- Date of service
- Amount charged and amount paid
- Your signature and the client's signature
- ICD-10 diagnosis codes
- CPT procedure codes

ICD-10 stands for "International Classification of Diseases, Version 10," and it is a classification system endorsed by the World Health Organization (WHO) that enables the definition, tracking, and monitoring of health conditions in a granular, universal way. You may be saying, "But I am not a licensed healthcare provider—diagnosing is not within my scope of practice." This is very true in a clinical sense. The IBCLC alone does not allow you to diagnose medical conditions. However, choosing an ICD-10 diagnosis code is not exactly the same thing as diagnosing a medical condition. Think of it like labeling the visit with a "why." The ICD-10 diagnosis explains the reason that services were provided. The definition of the diagnosis code Z39.1 is "encounter for care and exam of lactating mother," and this tends to be an appropriate diagnosis code for an IBCLC visit.

Procedure code is short for Current Procedure Terminology (CPT). These codes are used to communicate "what" happened during the visit. Here in the United States, insurance companies assign dollar amounts to each procedure code, and that is how payments and reimbursements are calculated. These amounts are not standardized but are subject to definition and application by the insurance companies, and there can be wide range of variation between one insurance company and the next.

Our services are considered preventive, and there is a set of CPT codes that is defined as preventive. These run from 99401 (15 minutes) through 99404 (60 minutes). These codes tend to reimburse at very low rates, but because they contain prevention within the definition of the code, they seem the most likely to trigger some reimbursement.

Code S9443 is defined as a 30-minute lactation class, but in some areas insurance providers are asking IBCLCs to use only that code on superbills. What this seems to mean is that you assign the full cost of your visit to S9443, essentially saying that a 30-minute breastfeeding class costs your full rate. You are not obligated to charge for staying longer than 30 minutes or for performing more services than the code encompasses. Keep in mind that this is not a rule or even a guideline, but a response to what some insurers have asked some IBCLCs in some areas. This code has also been known to pay at a very low rate from other carriers in other areas. It is one of the few CPT codes specific to lactation.

Evaluation and Management (E&M) codes tend to reimburse at the highest rates, but they are also the codes most likely to trigger a denial when you are out-of-network and/or do not have a medical license. These are time-based codes that also correspond with escalating levels of decision-making. Office visit codes start with 99201, and home-visit codes start with 99341. The higher you go, the more the code is worth, but you must be able to document in your charting the length of the visit and the level of complexity of the visit.

You will also be designating a location. If you see clients in your office, this is easy, just use location code 11. If you see clients in their own homes you probably use location code 12, but that's actually unclear. There is some debate over whether or not any home visit codes (location or E&M) are appropriate for IBCLC home visits, or if they are meant only for cases where a patient is physically restricted to their home as a result of their medical condition. Some recommend using the office codes even for home visit as if you are providing outpatient office services in the location of your choosing. Clear as mud, right?

On your superbill, you will also see areas where you can add modifiers. The most commonly used modifier is 33, which flags a code as preventive. If you use more than one code for a visit, modifier 25 links the two codes together into one visit.

You may want to purchase a pre-made superbill template, and I've listed sources below. Some charting platforms will generate superbills for you, but you will need to know your codes. My other book *Paperless Private Practice for Lactation Consultants* covers electronic options in depth.

Some insurance plans are "grandfathered," meaning they were in existence prior to the ACA and are exempt from ACA regulations. These clients may not get any reimbursement at all, and there isn't really anything you can do about it.

The Affordable Care Act and Insurance:
- Breastfeeding and the Affordable Care Act
- How else does the Affordable Care Act impact breastfeeding families?
- Breastfeeding Benefits from Healthcare.gov
- National Women's Law Center Breastfeeding Toolkit

Insurance Coding Resources:

- <u>What is ICD-10?</u>
- <u>WHO ICD Classifications</u>
- <u>Current Procedural Terminology</u>
- <u>Suggestions for Billing Codes for IBCLCs</u>
- <u>Crash Course in Coding, Documentation and Billing for In-Network IBCLCs</u>

Billing and Invoicing Forms:

- <u>Diana West's Superbills</u>
- <u>Pat Lindsay's Lactation Visit Receipt</u>
- <u>Professional paper claim form (CMS-1500)</u>

Insurance Contracts

At present, some insurance carriers in some areas are credentialing IBCLCs without another medical license. Aetna has been the pioneer, but in some states other insurers are bringing IBCLCs in-network. To apply to be in-network, you must contact the insurer directly or work with a biller who will make the application on your behalf. This may take time, and you may not be accepted if the insurer believes they have a sufficient amount of in-network providers.

When you are in-network with an insurance company, you agree to provide services to their members and accept what the insurance company will pay for the codes you submit. You are not permitted to charge your clients more than what the insurance company will pay you. For example, if you bill the insurance company $100 for code 99404 and they pay you $75, you may not send your client an invoice for $25. Some in-network IBCLCs work with lactation billers to help maximize payments and deal with the inevitable hassle when the insurance companies process claims incorrectly.

The Affordable Care Act stipulates that there should be no cost-sharing to families for preventive services, and lactation care is defined as a preventive service. Cost-sharing includes three types of charges that the insurance company may ask its members to pay directly to the provider:

- **Deductible**. This is a dollar amount the member is required to meet before the insurance company will pay certain claims.
- **Coinsurance**. Once the member has met their deductible, the insurance company may require the member to pay a percentage of the cost of visits and procedures.
- **Copay**. The insurance company may require the member to pay a certain dollar amount towards certain visits and procedures.

It is quite common for insurance companies to apply cost-sharing when processing claims, and some in-network IBCLCs with a high volume will hire professional billers to handle their initial claim submissions and reprocessing claims that have had cost-sharing applied. A professional biller will charge a flat fee for services or take a percentage on paid claims, or some combination of the two. Some billers will help you with your application to become a network provider, and some will even process out-of-network claims on behalf of your clients. Local or Facebook networking groups are a good place to get current recommendations on billers specializing in lactation.

Because we see two (or more) people during a lactation visit, an argument can be made that IBCLCs can also bill insurance providers on behalf of the baby, and that the baby's claim should also be considered preventive and therefore exempt from cost-sharing. In the majority of cases (prenatals being one notable exception), you must have a baby present in order to provide lactation care. If you must have a baby, then the baby's claim should be subject to ACA provisions just like the mother.

In reality, this argument doesn't always fly with the insurance companies. Sometimes they will pay the claim for the baby, sometimes they will apply it to the deductible, and sometimes they will apply coinsurance or a copay. When this happens, you are required by your in-network contract to bill the client for this amount. Once you send that invoice, what happens next is up to you as no one will be checking if you actually collect it. You are not prohibited from charging your client a fee to cover their baby's portion in the event that their baby has different insurance.

When you are in-network, you do have an obligation to see clients who carry that insurance, and you must be even more diligent in how you chart visits. I'll talk more about charting in a later chapter.

- Preventive Care
- Coinsurance
- Copays
- Lactation Support Services Coverage Under the Affordable Care Act
- Why Most Self-Employed Service Providers Can't Deduct Bad Business Debts
- Health Insurance Fraud
- The Challenge of Health Care Fraud

Bookkeeping and Filing Taxes

Your "books" refer to the system you use to keep track of your income (payments you receive from clients or from their insurance providers) and expenses (everything you spend on your business). Come tax time, you'll need to tell the Internal Revenue Service (IRS) all about your business activities, and pay the applicable taxes.

You can keep your own books (called "bookkeeping"), or work with a professional bookkeeper or accountant who focuses on small businesses. Similarly, you can file your own taxes or hire a professional to do them for you. If you have enough expenses that you will exceed the standard deduction for the tax year, you'll be itemizing all of your expenses in order to reduce the amount of taxes you are required to pay.

A good bookkeeping system can also generate what's called a Profit and Loss statement, where you can see if your business expenses are outpacing your income, and adjust accordingly. An accountant will know the tax code inside and out, and may be able to advise you on changes to make in your business structure in order to maximize the amount of income you can keep.

It's possible to keep books with pen and paper, or using a spreadsheet program like Google Sheets or Microsoft Excel. There are also a number of cloud-based accounting services available, and some will allow you to add your bookkeeper or accountant as part of your team.

If filing your own taxes, you can use an online or computer-based program, which will walk you through entering in the necessary information which the program will then use to generate your paperwork. Some of these online programs will provide accountants to review your forms before you submit them as an additional service.

Bookkeeping:

- The Best Small Business Accounting Software of 2018 (PC Mag)
- Best Small Business Accounting Software 2018 (Business News Daily)
- The 10 Best Accounting Software Solutions for Small Business
- The 8 Best Software Programs to Buy for Small Businesses in 2018
- Best Small Business Accounting Software

- Best Accounting Software for Small Business 2018: QuickBooks vs Xero vs Wave

Filing taxes:

- TaxAct vs. TurboTax 2018
- What's the Best Online Tax Preparation Software? TaxAct vs TurboTax vs H&R Block
- Four TurboTax Alternatives for Filing Your Tax Return
- The Best Tax Software

Communications Infrastructure

Your private practice is going to need a system in place to communicate with your clients and with your care providers, and because IBCLCs are subject to HIPAA, you will need to make sure that you are safeguarding Protected Health Information (PHI) in addition to keeping all client communications confidential. I recommend my book *Paperless Private Practice for Lactation Consultants* for a deeper dive into electronic communications.

- Paperless Lactation
- Communications Services Comparison Chart
- Making Good Choices About Using Email, Text, Voice, and Apps with Clients
- Clients Have the Right to Receive Unencrypted Emails (and Texts) Under HIPAA

Phone

Nothing really beats the phone for client communications. When you use a landline or your cell phone, you're not subject to any HIPAA considerations, and a separate landline on traditional carrier with its own answering machine is the simplest path towards keeping your work life and your personal life separated.

You may want to run your business from a mobile phone, and the best practice is to have a separate mobile phone for work. There are services that will allow you to have a second line on the same phone using Voice Over Internet Protocol (VoIP), and you will need to contract with a provider that will offer you a Business Associate Agreement (BAA) so that you are meeting your obligations under HIPAA. This also applies if you hire a third party to act as a receptionist, such as a virtual assistant or an answering service.

Whenever you speak to your clients on the phone, it's important to take precautions to protect their confidentiality. The easiest way to do this is to make client phone calls in an office with the door closed, or while alone in your car. Because cell phones make it possible to take phone calls anywhere, it can be tempting to return client phone calls while pumping gas or while sitting in a waiting room, but if others are in earshot while you are on the phone, you are violating your client's privacy.

It's possible to run your private practice with only a phone, but there are some limitations. Phone calls have to happen when both parties are awake, whereas messaging, email, and texting can take place at any time of day or night. You need to document all phone calls, and it's hard to give links to online resources over the phone. Some IBCLCs include phone follow-up as part of their consult fee, others charge for phone calls, and some IBCLCs do not include phone follow-up at all.

- HIPAA and "VoIP" Services
- 6 Tips for Phones for Private Practice

Secure Messaging

The best practice for communicating with your clients is in a secure messaging environment. You may have heard of popular platforms like WhatsApp or Signal or similar, and wonder how they are different from SMS or cloud-based messaging services like iCloud.

The primary draw of secure messaging platforms is end-to-end end encryption. Basically, using SMS or iCloud for texting/messaging is like having a phone conversation on a street corner. Probably nobody is actually listening to you, but if someone wanted to, they could. Upgrading to secure messaging is like stepping inside a soundproofed chamber and closing the door. Nobody can listen even if they wanted to.

The final consideration for healthcare providers is what access the app has to any PHI stored on your device, and here is where many platforms fall apart. If the service accesses your contacts, your calendar, or your location, you need a BAA in place. This is bad news, because in most cases this means you are going to have to pay.

If you use an all-in-one Electronic Health Records (EHR) platform for charting client visits and storing their information, these systems often come with secure messaging built in. Most of the HIPAA-compliant VoIP solutions include secure messaging in the platform, so if you plan to get a second line for your private practice this can be a cost-effective way to go. You could also use a standalone messaging app that meets HIPAA requirements or offers a BAA.

On your end, these systems are all relatively straightforward to use once you get them set up. The primary issue is compliance—from your clients. Because your relationship with them may span a relatively short time, they may not want to create a login or download an app just to communicate with you. If they only see you once, and then decide to reach out to you several months later, they may even forget that secure messaging is an option.

Setting up secure messaging with your clients in advance of the visit can be key for compliance. When booking the visit, consider inviting them right then and there, and then when you exchange texts about the appointment time (such as reminders), they can take place in a secure environment and "train" your client to interact with you within the secure environment. In order to truly achieve secure messaging compliance, you will need to set limits with your clients about how you will communicate with them. Reminding them that you have these policies in place for their protection and because the law requires it can help people understand the necessity of secure messaging.

When you have a conversation with your client using secure messaging, you will need to save it, either by documenting in your client's chart or through a platform that automatically saves conversations.

Decide in advance whether you will include follow-up by messaging in the fee your clients pay you for a visit, and how long that follow up will last. Setting limits in advance will pave the way for smoother relationships with your clients, and allows you to have boundaries that can prevent burnout and compassion fatigue.

Please note that the messaging features in social media platforms like Facebook, Twitter, Instagram, and the like are never appropriate for client communications. It is impossible to control privacy to a HIPAA-compliant degree because privacy violation is a feature of these platforms, not a bug. Do not grant social media accounts access to your calendar or contacts if you use them for any PHI.

I update my website frequently with resources to help you choose the communications system that meets your specific needs

- Secure Messaging Demystified
- Secure Messaging Showdown: WhatsApp vs. Signal – this article contains a terrific explanation of how secure messaging works, and also highlights some of the privacy concerns that make them potentially inappropriate for healthcare usage

- <u>Clients Have the Right to Receive Unencrypted Emails (and Texts) Under HIPAA</u>
- <u>Even Though They Have a Right Under HIPAA To Unencrypted Emails: A Case For Only Using Secure Email and Texting With Clients</u>
- <u>Apps You Can Use To Create Highly Private Spaces Online for Clients</u>
- <u>How Effective is Secure Messaging in Healthcare?</u>

Text

If you end up using a smartphone for work, you will then be able to send and receive texts via your work phone number. This is super helpful for booking appointments, especially for last-minute ones, and can help you respond as quickly as possible to new appointment requests.

Because it is so easy to use, text does have significant drawbacks. Potential clients will text you all kinds of Protected Health Information (PHI). I've gotten texts inquiring about an appointment that contain full name, address, date of birth, and insurance ID number. Now, you're not responsible for unsolicited PHI from people with whom you do not have a client relationship, but you do have to manage your texting relationship with your clients in a way that respects your obligations under HIPAA, maintains healthy limits, and supports them in self-efficacy.

Current clients will still text you even if you tell them you want them to use secure messaging—even if they have gone the extra step and set up a secure messaging account with your practice. They will simply forget or will not be bothered to use it. Honestly, who can blame them? They just had a baby! Just because they text you doesn't mean you have to text them back. You can call them, send an email, or use your secure messaging platform to respond to their texts.

A bigger issue with texting is the sense of urgency that a text can create. When a client texts details on a problem they are having, you may feel the need to respond right away and then things spiral out of control. Here's an example:

Client: the baby is crying all the time, he's not getting enough

IBCLC: how many wet and dirty diapers is he having?

Client: he's just so hungry, I don't have enough milk

Client: he just guzzled a bottle of formula

Client: he is starving

IBCLC: is he peeing and pooping?

Client: What am I going to do if I can't breastfeed?

Client: I don't have enough milk

IBCLC: can you tell me how many wet and dirty diapers he's having?

Client: every time he eats

Client: I can't listen to him cry

IBCLC: how often is he eating?

Client: how can I increase my milk supply?

Client: what herbs can I take?

Client: he just won't last three hours between feedings, he gets so hungry between

Client: because I don't have enough milk

IBCLC: (scrambles to find resources on feeding frequency and scheduled feedings while client keeps texting)

This kind of text exchange happens so frequently in our work, and very rarely does it seem to help. A better response would be to write, "I got your text and you sound really overwhelmed. I'm so glad you contacted me. I'm sending you an email, look for it later today." In the email, list out the questions you need the client to answer for you to assess her situation and respond to their questions. This will slow down the conversation and remove some of the urgency. By feeding the urgency, you may be preventing your client from assimilating the information that will lead to self-efficacy.

Another option is call the client back and have this conversation over the phone. They will get the opportunity to share her frustrations, and while you listen and validate their feelings, you can gather the information you need and formulate a response that builds on the care plan.

Any text interactions will need to be documented and that record kept with your client's chart, because SMS texts are not stored anywhere permanently the way secure messages can be stored. iMessage is not suitable for client communications because at the time of writing Apple will not provide a BAA.

- Policy Statement: Texting and Healthcare
- How to Stop Clients from Invading Your After-Hours Time (not healthcare specific)
- 3 Ways Texting with Clients Can Hurt Your Business (not healthcare specific)
- 6 simple rules to live by when texting clients (this article is for real estate agents but I think these principles are great ones for us to consider)

Email

I am old enough to remember when email was magic, not a tiresome requirement for modern life. You really can't do anything of substance online without an email address, and most of us have at least one if not more. Email is an expedient way to communicate a written care plan to your clients, and it's convenient for communicating with other healthcare providers.

You will want to have an email address that is separate from any personal addresses you may have. In order to manage your email in a HIPAA-secure way, you will need to create an email address with a provider who will give you a BAA. I'm sorry to say this means no free Gmail, but don't worry—you have options. My book *Paperless Private Practice for Lactation Consultants* walks you through how to create and use a HIPAA-secure email system.

Use professionalism in any written correspondence with your clients. You want your emails to be clear, direct, and free from excessive wordiness. Refrain from including details about your own personal life. While generally it's a good idea to avoid emojis and exclamation points, you may find that the most appropriate response to an email is: "Yeah!! I'm so happy to hear that! You're amazing ☺"

A risk to having an email address that you post publicly on your website is that you may receive emails where the appointment request also includes a bunch of questions about the situation at hand. Troubleshooting breastfeeding issues via email with someone creates a clinical relationship with them, and makes you responsible for dealing with them as you would deal with any client. You have to create a chart for them, you need them to sign a consent form, and you need to be mindful of HIPAA when communicating with them. That is a lot of work for someone who is not your client. Keep it simple and never be afraid to say that you cannot answer their question without seeing them in person. As Elizabeth Brooks, JD IBCLC often posts in IBCLC Facebook groups— "step away from the mini consult!"

- Email and HIPAA Compliant Practice: Is It Possible?
- Email Tips for Clinicians
- I Love These Emails, Or Do I?
- Psychologists Use of E-mail with Clients: Some Ethical Considerations

- The Woman Who Couldn't Stop Emailing. And The Therapist Who Got Sucked In

Fax

Fax? Really? Isn't that like the Pony Express of telecommunications? Unfortunately, many medical offices are not yet equipped to receive and send emails from other providers, so in most cases when you want to send a report to your client's pediatrician, OB, or midwife, you'll need to send it by fax.

To send a fax, you scan a document into a fax machine and dial a fax number to connect your machine to another fax machine over telephone wires. Your fax machine will transmit the image of your document to that fax machine, and it will print on the other end. You will get a confirmation when your fax is successfully received. Because faxes cannot be easily intercepted or altered while en-route, they are considered a HIPAA-compliant means of electronic transmission.

You can purchase a fax machine and sign up for a dedicated fax number through your local phone company. Many of these machines are also scanners, printers, and copiers and can be a useful tool. If you aspire to a paperless practice, look into email-to-fax solutions, as many will offer you a BAA.

Before transmitting a fax to an office for the first time, you should send a test fax and confirm with a phone call that it has been received. This is a safeguard against unintentionally transmitting PHI to an unknown recipient.

- Why Are Fax Machines Still a Thing?
- Why Your Doctor Still Relies on Fax Machines
- The Fax of Life

Telemedicine

Telemedicine or telehealth has been touted as the future of healthcare. Instead of having to leave your house to see a doctor in your geographical vicinity, you can stay in the comfort of your own home and consult with a specialist from another part of the country or the world, all thanks to the wonders of video-based communications. It used to be that the idea of seeing someone's face while talking with them on the phone was something you only saw in a science fiction movie; now it's entirely commonplace.

There are many IBCLCs incorporating telemedicine into their private practices, as an additional income stream in areas with low population density, or because they have an area of specialty that sets them apart from others. The upside is that you can increase your client base without adding to your travel time. The downside is that you are limited to what you can observe with your eyes and ears through a computer screen. You cannot perform an oral exam on an infant, and you cannot palpate a parent's glandular tissue. You cannot use touch to adjust positioning, and you cannot provide hands-on instruction in the use of a device such as an at-breast supplementer. You can provide counseling, information, support, and resources, making telemedicine ideal for prenatal consults, back-to-work education, and support related to the normal course of breastfeeding.

If you are considering incorporating telemedicine into your practice, you will need to offer it through a HIPAA-compliant platform. Do not FaceTime or Skype or Google Hangout with your clients—none of these platforms will give you a BAA. Some EHR platforms include telemedicine as an included or add-on feature, enabling you to chart during a telehealth visit. At the time of writing, Google will provide a BAA for Meet, though their video options do seem to keep shifting and changing. There are some services that will hire healthcare providers to offer telemedicine through their interface, and some have been hiring IBCLCs.

What if your client insists that they are fine with the privacy risks of a non-secure platform? You still have to offer them a secure option so they can give true consent to opt out. Think of it like this—if your doctor said, "I do not have an office. The only way I can see you is if you meet me on a street corner," your doctor is basically forcing you to give up your privacy with no alternatives. But if they say, "You can come to my office in three days and have complete privacy, or I can meet you on a street corner at 7:30 tonight with no guarantee of privacy." You are now able to give true consent because you understand the options and were given a reasonable alternative. Your client will either accept the inconvenience of using a secure platform, or waive their privacy in order to use the platform of their choice. Then, you document that the secure option was offered and the client declined.

You may still feel that you are not comfortable using a non-secure platform; you are not obligated to offer your client telemedicine at all so you are free to decline those services if your client is unwilling to use a secure platform.

- The Impact Of HIPAA On Telemedicine
- Telemedicine Legal Series: HIPAA
- Free, HIPAA-Secure Online Therapy Software (2018 Update)
- Is My Telehealth App Subject to HIPAA?
- Keeping Telemedicine HIPAA Compliant
- Using Videoconferencing Technology to Provide Breastfeeding Support to Low-Income Women: Connecting Hospital-Based Lactation Consultants with Clients Receiving Care at a Community Health Center

Charting Infrastructure

As mentioned above, you will be taking a history and documenting every encounter you have with your clients, including those communications that take place by phone, text, email, or telemedicine.

In order to chart, you will need a system, the necessary supplies, and secure storage. You can chart on paper, electronically, or through some combination of the two. You can purchase charts made by other IBCLCs (like mine) or develop your own. You can enroll with an practice management system, also known as an EHR (Electronic Health Record) platform, or create your own electronic system. There's nothing stopping you from having file folders with paper checklists and hard copy resources in a locked filing cabinet.

The benefits of electronic charting include portability, no physical storage required, and integrations that facilitate client and provider communications. The potential downsides are the learning curve for mastering a new technology that may not perform in a way that is intuitive to you, and the issue of having a screen between you and your client. You may have experienced this yourself—the doctor's visit where nobody makes eye contact with you because they're so busy checking boxes on a screen. Mindfulness is essential when using electronic charting during a visit; setting the screen aside to give your full attention to your client and their baby is always the priority. Using a portable device like a tablet or laptop can help during a home or office visit, because you can put it down anywhere. If you are in an office and use a desktop computer, consider placing your computer so that it doesn't become a physical barrier between you and your clients. For electronic charting, you will need:

- Computer, tablet, or smartphone
- Scanner (portable or all-in-one)
- Shredder
- Internet connection
- Mobile hotspot if you do home visits and your system doesn't have offline access
- Cloud-based storage with a BAA for client files

- Charting templates

Paper charting may make it easier to pay attention to your client, as it can be easier to set aside a clipboard than a computer. It may also seem more cost-effective, compared to the subscription fees to use an EHR platform or the costs to purchase a mobile device or computer. However, paper and ink for printing can add up to a substantial amount, meaning that paper charting may not be the most cost-effective solution. Paper also takes up space, and if your client loses a paper handout you will have to consider how to get her a replacement copy. For paper charting, you will need:

- Clipboard
- Pens
- Manila folders
- Locked storage cabinet
- Fax machine
- Charting templates
- Printer/copier or access to printing and copying services

You can also combine paper and electronic charting, which many IBCLCs still do. It is possible to be nearly 100 percent paperless in your private practice, save for the paper that comes from outside sources like insurance companies or other healthcare providers.

- Diana West's Clinical Forms
- G-Suite for IBCLCs
- Milk Notes
- Mobile Lactation Consultant
- EHR Comparison Chart for IBCLCs
- What Happens if Your Physical Therapy Software Goes Out of Business?

Physical Supplies

In order to perform assessments and provide interventions to your clients and their babies, you will need certain supplies on hand.

Latex-free exam gloves. You will always be using gloves whenever performing an oral assessment on a baby. You may or may not use gloves when assessing the parent's breasts. Many people are allergic to latex, and you would not want to risk a reaction in an infant, so make sure you choose the latex-free gloves.

Scale. If you are performing pre- and post-feed weights as part of your clinical assessment, you will need a scale with a very high degree of precision and accuracy. At the time of writing, the most popular scales for IBCLCs are the Tanita BD-815U, the Medela Baby Weigh II, and the Marsden M-300. Do not let price tempt you into a less-expensive model; those scales can have significant variations from weight to weight, rendering them unable to provide a trustworthy calculation of intake. Many of these scales come with carrying cases, or you could use a large rolling suitcase. I always make sure I have extra batteries for my scale, especially because I have left my scale's A/C adapter behind on more than one occasion.

Supplies. To every visit I bring an assortment of nipple shields and breast pump flanges in various sizes, tubing and syringes for finger feeding, containers for hand expression collection, silicone milk collector, Lact-Aid at-breast supplementer, Medela pump gauge, Supple Cups, an auscultator, and a small flashlight for oral exams. If you are giving supplies to your clients, you will need to decide if you are charging them or if you are putting the cost towards your business expenses.

Miscellaneous. I always have breath mints for when it's time to get close, fragrance-free hand soap, and hand sanitizer. I have my card reader for my online payment system, and business cards with my contact information.

- <u>Selecting and Using Breastfeeding Tools by Catherine Watson Genna</u>
- <u>What's in your Pandora's-box-of-an-IBCLC home-visiting bag?</u>
- <u>Business Advice for Private Practice Lactation Consultants: Rachel's Home Visit Supply Kit</u>

Policies and Procedures Manual

Now that you have created your business entity, set up all your essential elements, created your infrastructure, and ordered your supplies, it's time to create your Policies and Procedures manual. Basically, this is a document that tells the world who you are and how you do things. If you hire any employees, your Policies and Procedures manual contains all of your human resources policies. Write it all down, and have it somewhere accessible. Because I am not a lawyer, I recommend working with your own legal counsel to make sure your Policies and Procedures manual meets all the necessary requirements and doesn't unintentionally expose you to risk.

What are recommended topics to include?

Contact information and identification:

- Company name, credentials, and applicable licenses
- Company contact information
- Vision statement
- Business structure and components
- Business structure, as in LLC or sole proprietorship
- EIN
- NPI

Legal forms and contracts:

- Liability insurance carrier and policy number

- Legal forms
- Consent for Care
- Notice of Privacy Practices
- Rental Agreement (if you rent pumps or scales)
- Business Associates Agreement
- Subcontractor Agreement (if applicable)
- Zoning licenses (if applicable)

Payment policies:

- Fee structure and payment policies
- Initial and follow up visits
- Additional fees (travel, etc.)
- Additional services (phone Consults, telemedicine)
- Payment methods accepted
- Insurance accepted (if any)
- Sliding scale terms
- Packages
- Discounts
- Pump and scale rentals
- Retail offerings
- Cancellation policy

Appointment definitions and parameters:

- Appointment definitions
- Type of appointment
- Where the appointment takes place
- Duration of appointment
- Overview of a typical appointment
- How to schedule an appointment
- How client prepares

- How intake is completed
- What's included in fee for visit
- Policy on pets (for home visits)
- Follow-up policies
- What's included in fee for visit
- Expiration date
- Who initiates—you or client?

Communication policies:

- Phone
- Secure messaging
- Email
- Text
- Social media policies
- HIPAA compliance measures implemented
- Reporting
- Who gets reports from you
- If you are a mandated reporter

Documentation policies:

- Charting infrastructure
- HIPAA compliance measures implemented
- Record storage policies
- HIPAA compliance measures implemented
- Chart access procedure for clients

Office policies:

- Office location
- Office hours

Ethics:

- WHO Code compliance measures implemented
- Gift policies

Employee policies:

- Reporting workplace discrimination
- Vacation/sick day policy
- Social media for employees
- Communication policies for employees
- Dress code
- Break time
- Provisions for lactating employees
- Subcontractors
- Definition of working relationships
- Payment/compensation structure

Intern/mentorship policies:

- If you offer mentorship for supervised clinical hours
- Terms of internship

Business partnership policies:

- Business partners
- Terms of the partnership
- Ownership stake in the company
- Exit clause

Notice I have not gone into much detail about how to write the manual. That's because you will need to develop these policies yourself according to the way you work. This list is not comprehensive; there may be elements specific to your practice that I have not mentioned here. Not all of these topics will apply to you. An attorney is the best person to review your Policies and Procedures Manual before you publish it.

- International Code of Marketing of Breast-Milk Substitutes
- The Policy and Procedure Manual: Managing "By the Book"
- How do I Develop a Policy & Procedures Manual?
- First Things First: Office Policies for Your Consideration
- Policies and Procedures Manuals
- How to Start Creating Your Policies and Procedures Manual
- How to write a Policies and Procedures Manual
- Sample Human Resources Policies and Procedures
- Understanding HIPAA Security Policies and Procedures

Launch

Now for the fun part—getting your baby out into the world. In this section, I'll cover various strategies for making your presence known in the wider world.

- What Is the Difference Between Advertising & Promotion
- Difference Between Advertising and Promotion
- 7 Free Strategies to Market Your Private Practice
- Free Publicity? By Nancy Mohrbacher
- 7 Ways to Attract Clients to Your Birth Business
- 10 Ways to Promote Your Doula Business for Free or Super Cheap!
- Why content marketing is perfect for midwives and doulas

Publicity

Publicity encompasses the ways in which you share your services, identity, and brand with the wider world. Promotional tools create a public identity designed to increase your customer base.

Website

Your website is your virtual business card and is the most important promotional tool at your disposal. Someone coming to your website should be able to learn everything they need to know about you, your fees and policies, what happens during a visit, and how to contact you. Having a physical business card is often still the best way to provide your contact information to pediatricians and other healthcare professionals. The business card is easier to create, but you may want to start with your website as a way to develop a visual identity that can translate into a physical card.

Unless you have a passion for web development and design, the easiest way to create a website will be to go through a provider who will sell you a domain name, host your website, and offer design templates that you can customize yourself. At the time of writing, the three biggest players are Wix, Weebly, and SquareSpace. Wordpress.org is another popular service with seemingly unlimited templates and add-ons, but you'll have to get your domain name and hosting separately (with Wordpress holding your hand).

Ideally, your domain name is your business name or your full name. Using identifiable words like "lactation" or "IBCLC" in your domain name boosts your searchability and makes it easier for potential clients to find you through search engines. That said, if you have a business name you're in love with, then go for it. There are other ways to add search engine optimization into your web design, through adding metadata and keywords. When you use a template from a provider like SquareSpace, for example, if you poke around you will find places where you can add words that aren't visible on your site but that can be discovered by search engine bots, or computer scripts that crawl over websites gathering search terms.

When choosing a design template for your website, you will want to make sure that it's optimized for mobile viewing. That means that the layout will change if the website senses that the visitor is using the browser on their phone or tablet. Not having a mobile-friendly website can actually be detrimental to your business, as a visitor may wonder if your website is outdated then maybe your clinical skills will be outdated, too.

The goal of any website is a what's known as a conversion. You want people visiting your website to do something, so you want your website to make that clear with a call-to-action. "Call/text for an appointment" followed by your phone number. "Contact me" followed by your phone number and email address. Your template should convert any contact information you post into links that launch the person's dialpad or email client, and if that's not happening when you test the live site, use the help pages or customer service to find out what you need to do. "Book now" if you use an online scheduling service like Acuity or through your EHR platform.

A simple tagline explaining your services is vitally important. Not only will it explain what you do, but it will provoke an immediate response—leave or act—and will also include search terms. Mine is "Home Visits for Breastfeeding Support Queens/Brooklyn." You either want that or you don't. However, if you're competing in a crowded market you may want your tagline to do more to differentiate yourself and your practice style or area of specialty. Look at what other IBCLCs are doing with their websites to take what works and leave the rest, then come up with an original tagline that best serves your purposes.

When it comes to design, you may be highly skilled or completely lost. Many IBCLCs will hire someone to design a logo and come up with a color scheme so that all their elements are uniform throughout. Selecting a font can be overwhelming because of all the choices, so a professional designer may be a good person to help with that, too. Looking at lots of other websites will help you identify trends and discern what stylistic choices speak to you. The colors, images, and fonts you choose can then also be translated into your physical business card.

Keep your design simple and focused on the services you provide. People don't tend to read a lot of text, and forget about any background animation or music. If there's too much clutter, people will get overwhelmed and may end up looking for someone else with a cleaner website. If you have a logo, use it judiciously throughout, and see if your template will allow you to use it to replace the graphic that appears in the URL bar, called a favicon.

You must respect copyright and intellectual property. If you need photos for your website, you will need to either own them or purchase them, and if they're photos of your clients you need to have written permission to use their likenesses in your promotional materials. You can purchase stock photos from many different websites, but you will always need to check the terms of usage to make sure you are allowed to use the photo on your website. I would encourage you to search for images that represent the spectrum of human appearances, so that someone coming to your website will not just see dominant (white) culture represented visually.

You may read something that you absolutely love on another IBCLCs website. Do not copy and paste that text, even if you give credit. It is not yours; it belongs to that IBCLC. You can ask permission to use it, and that IBCLC can grant permission, deny permission, or charge you a fee for permission. The point is that it's up to the person who wrote that text, and using it without permission is in violation of the IBLCE Code of Professional Conduct. If you go even further and pretend you wrote it, that's plagiarism.

Web design:

- <u>8 Effective Web Design Principles You Should Know</u>
- <u>10 Principles Of Good Website Design</u>
- <u>10 Principles of Basic Web Design</u>
- <u>What Makes a Good Mobile Site?</u>
- <u>How to Pick the Perfect Font Style Design for your Website</u>

- Font Recommendations & Lists
- Canva Alternatives: 8 More Simple Graphic Design Tools

Legal issues:

- Website Legal Forms Pack
- The 3 Key Legal Policies You Need To Protect Your Online Hub
- Does my website really need a Terms and Conditions page?

Stock photos:

- Looking for free public domain images? Here are the best websites to find them
- Free & Paid Sources for Doula Stock Photos

Search Engine Optimization:

- Search Engine Optimization: Its Goals, Techniques & How SEO Works
- SEO basics: 22 essentials you need for optimizing your site

Business Cards

After creating your website, choose the visual elements that will translate to the small format of your business card. The business card's primary function is to provide your contact information in a wallet-sized format. It needs to have your name, credentials, website, phone number, email address, and your tagline. Your logo can go on your card as well.

If you speak any languages other than the dominant one in your area, your business card is a good place to indicate that, too. If you are fluent in another language, creating additional cards in that language as a way to let immigrant families know that they can receive support in their native tongue. Being able to relax and not have to translate can mean so much to an overwhelmed postpartum family, and using their language creates a safe space for them.

Some IBCLCs use the back of their business cards as a referral box, where a pediatrician or other care provider can indicate their name and the reason(s) they are referring their patient to see an IBCLC. Another use for the back of the card is listing clinic or support group days/times, but if these are subject to change you may just want to list your website so you're not having to order new business cards every time the yoga studio hosting your group changes their schedule.

- Best Business Card Provider for Small Businesses 2018
- Best 25 Places to Buy Small Business Cards

Other Promotional Materials

With a logo and a tagline, you have what you need to delve into the world of giveaways and freebies. I've seen everything from t-shirts to car decals to flashlights topped by a breast. The sky is the limit for what you can design as a promotional tool, but because you'll be spending money, consider your goals carefully. Who would wear that t-shirt? Will that flashlight just get thrown away? Will anyone even notice that car decal?

Before you choose your tool, decide what outcome you are trying to provoke. If you want to get your name in front of the most popular pediatrician in town, a free pen or pad of post-it notes can be effective. Looking to raise your profile in your local birthing and postpartum community? An Instagrammable novelty item may be just what you need. And if your hope is that satisfied clients will tell their friends about you, maybe a branded stainless steel water bottle will help spread the love. Save the t-shirts for your partners, interns, and business associates, unless you have a killer design that someone would wear even if they've never breastfed a day in their life.

There are non-tangible ways to promote your business as well, such as sponsoring an event like a 5K raising money for a birth- or postpartum-related cause, purchasing a booth at a local baby fair, or partnering with another professional to offer a community event like a lecture or a meetup.

And to be honest, marketing gimmicks may end up doing absolutely nothing for you. Face-to-face connections, like those you establish with your colleagues and other healthcare providers, will likely turn out to be a more valuable source of client referrals than any box of pens you could buy. That said, don't underestimate the power of putting your name out there in the world in a fun and unique way.

- The Pros & Cons of Free Gift Campaigns
- 6 Reasons Giving Away Free Stuff Can Work For Your Small Business
- Are Tote Bags Really Good for the Environment?

Advertising

Advertising generally refers to a paid campaign targeting a specific call to action. In the private practice world, this often means online advertising; specifically, through Google AdWords (which serves ads with Google searches and inside other Google products) but also on social media sites.

However, print ads are still very much a thing; for example, buying ad space in a publication geared towards local parents can be an effective way to advertise your services. Additionally, paying for a listing on the resource page for a local birth or breastfeeding network, alliance, or professional association can be the most effective money you can spend.

I'm going to make a true confession here—while I've used Google AdWords and consider myself pretty tech-savvy, I find everything about the Google AdWords interface to be confusing, overwhelming, and impossible to navigate. Somehow I managed to set up some keywords and I periodically get emails suggesting I do some tuneups, but I think there's a reason that there are so many books and products on the market to explain how to make AdWords work for you.

Basically, with AdWords you create a short advertisement of a few lines with a strict character limit, then you tie that ad to relevant keywords that you think people will be searching for. As a very rudimentary example, an ad could just be your tagline, phone number, and website, and you can tie that to keywords like "breastfeeding," "lactation," "bad latch," "tongue tie," and keywords for your the neighborhoods, towns, and counties in your service area. Then, you tell Google how much you want to spend each month on advertising. This is where it gets impenetrable, because Google makes all kinds of calculations about how much each click is worth and understanding that valuation isn't easy. It seems like your only choices are to take a deep dive and read all the books, or trust the process.

Facebook also allows you to create ads. You'll need a Facebook Page for your private practice, preferably publishing content on a somewhat regular basis. Facebook ads can be hit or miss, but certainly worth investigating. More on using social media for self-promotion in an upcoming section.

- The 3 Important Steps to Make AdWords Work for Your Private Practice
- Should I be using Google AdWords to grow my private practice?
- Facebook Ads

Networking

Fundamentally, networking means connecting with other professionals in related or adjacent professions for the purpose of growing your business. For IBCLCs, this primarily means meeting other IBCLCs, as well as childbirth educators, doulas, pediatricians, frenotomy providers, bodyworkers, acupuncturists, herbalists, physical therapists, speech/language pathologists, and therapists specializing in perinatal mood disorders.

Notice that I put other IBCLCs at the top of the list. "But aren't they my competition?" Yes, but only sort of. Our profession faces many obstacles that can limit the market for our services, but I believe by working together to overcome these barriers we can create a bigger market with room for all. The more people who value breastfeeding, the more our role will be valued.

I practice in a very dense geographic area; specifically, Queens and Brooklyn in New York City. Our local chapter of USLCA is called NYLCA, and we have a Facebook group where we share information, events, and mutual support. We also have a WhatsApp group for referrals when we're not available. For example, a family will reach out to me for help but I'm totally booked, so I get their location and post in the WhatsApp group something like "Family in Jackson Heights needs home visit—who's available?" I pass responses back to the family. Your local chapter of NYLCA or of the US Breastfeeding Committee may be a great place to start if your area doesn't already have a referral network in place.

In New York City, it seems like demand for IBCLCs outpaces our overall availability. But you may live in an area that is more spread out with a lower population overall, and perhaps there are only a few of you serving your area. It may feel like it's a race to answer the phone when a potential client calls, and that can fuel a feeling of competition with the other IBCLCs in your area. Networking with those other IBCLCs may in fact increase client volume for all of you, as together you may come up with outreach strategies specific to your geographic area. I am a firm believer that collaboration creates opportunities.

Some of you may be the only IBCLC for miles and miles and wish you had a competitor you could convert into a colleague. But you have nobody to share your struggles. In that case, there are many online resources for virtual networking, mostly on Facebook, and I'll provide them in the resources list at the end of this chapter.

Birth workers like childbirth educators and doulas can be terrific referral sources, and are a great place to target your networking efforts when you are getting started. Because of the trust they have developed with their clients, doulas are particularly influential in guiding families towards hiring an IBCLC. Help them get to know you and make an in-person connection to develop trust and confidence in the services you provide.

Pediatricians are a funny lot, aren't they? Some of them love us, some of them tolerate us, and some of them basically think we are witches. It's worth trying to win them over, because a pediatrician who will give out your name can send a lot of potential clients your way. Your care plans can be a powerful tool for demonstrating your competence and skills (more on how to write those later), but nothing beats an in-person meeting. Make an appointment to introduce yourself and explain what you can offer to their patients. You may even be so bold as to ask, "What might prevent you from referring your patients to an IBCLC?"

Bodyworkers, frenotomy providers, and chiropractors provide services so interconnected with the work we do that it's critical we cultivate meaningful relationships with those in our geographic area. Don't rely on word of mouth to tell you who's worth referring to—make those connections yourself, and make them personally. Spend a day shadowing the frenotomy provider; schedule your own self-care session with the bodyworker.

It may take some effort to discover the best people in your area to provide your families with the support they need, but it's always going to be worth it. Many of these relationships become mutually profitable, with reciprocal referrals. Wherever possible, work on having 2-3 names in each category to avoid any potential conflict of interest or appearance of bias. If there truly is only one person in your geographic area who you trust with a particular service, make sure you communicate with your clients why you are unable to offer alternatives. Reliance on one provider can backfire on everyone, because if there's disagreement, conflict, or even one unsatisfied client, you may not be able to address it directly for fear of the ramifications to your other clients if the referral relationship is strained or severed.

- Here's How To Build A Win-Win Networking Relationship
- 3 Ways to Network Your Way to Genuine Relationships
- How Introverts Can Network Powerfully: 5 Key Ways To Rock At Networking When You Hate It
- Top 8 Career Networking Tips for Introverts
- USLCA
- USBC
- Canadian Lactation Consultant Association
- LCinPP Conference – annual conference in Philadelphia exclusively for private practice. Once you register for your first conference, you can join their immensely valuable Facebook group. And don't wait to go, many of us feel it is the highlight of our professional year.

Social media

Honestly, this is possibly my absolute least favorite topic in the whole world. Like many of you, I have a love-hate relationship with Facebook. I cannot fathom working in private practice without my professional Facebook groups, yet I'm utterly envious of my friends and loved ones who just don't do Facebook at all. I'm aware of the ways in which social media is engineered to create addiction, and am periodically reminded that I'm giving up mindfulness in the quest for connection. Yet I persist.

At the time of this writing, the major social media platforms include Facebook, Instagram (owned by Facebook), Twitter, and Pinterest. Because social media changes and evolves so rapidly, I am not going to go into specific detail about how to make individual platforms work for you. Instead, I am going to offer principles towards effective social media usages that limit your risk for violating HIPAA or client confidentiality.

For the private practice IBCLC, social media can be a powerful tool for promoting your services and your personal style. With a Facebook page, you can have a free online presence that can link directly to your website, and where you can post helpful resources and engage in breastfeeding advocacy. On Twitter, you can share news stories with your audience, and with Instagram you can share images that promote breastfeeding success stories (get explicit permission before sharing any photos of your clients). A Pinterest collection can showcase inspirational imagery and informative resources in a visually appealing way. With all of these platforms you'll be able to connect with other professionals, both local and international, for support, collaboration, and professional development.

The pitfalls with social media are inherent in the name itself—the social aspect is what can bring you to your knees. I'm going to run through a few common social media scenarios, explain why they are problematic, and offer suggestions for a compassionate and ethical workaround.

For starters, don't allow your social media accounts to have access to your contacts, calendar, or location. Social media is engineered to leverage your relationships and your activities into new connections. If you store any PHI in the contacts file on your phone, and you allow your social media account to have access to your contacts, then anyone on either of your friends lists can see that you and your client have a relationship. This is a HIPAA breach because you have exposed your client's name, which is PHI. These social media platforms are constantly updating their terms of service and will do everything in their power to make you let them see your contacts, so it's critical to prevent that link from happening. If you have already allowed your social media account to have access to your contacts and that account has been able to "see" any PHI, ask your attorney about appropriate next steps. HIPAA requires that you notify your clients of any breach.

Your clients may send you friend or connection requests through social media. Before thinking "yay, baby pictures," consider very closely the potential ramifications of allowing your clients in to your personal life. What if you find that you have diametrically opposed positions on deeply held political, religious, or personal beliefs? Will that lead your client to question the care they received from you? Will those lifestyle differences cause them to hesitate before recommending you to another family?

Perhaps you know that you and this client are two peas in a pod when it comes to politics and religion. Before accepting a request from a client, you are obligated to inform them that you will be unable to protect their PHI if you connect on social media, and obtain explicit consent for any sharing of PHI that happens on a social media platform. Finally, advise them that you will not offer them any clinical support or breastfeeding information through social media, and refer them back to your follow-up policies. This can all be done in a friendly way, and I have email scripts for sale in my store.

Facebook groups are a particularly menacing minefield. In parent groups in posts asking for a lactation consultant, your clients will tag you and say, "Annie Frisbie helped us," or (hopefully rarely), "Annie Frisbie was not helpful at all." What do you do when that happens? Do not respond, I repeat, DO NOT respond. Just because your client is publicly acknowledging a relationship does not mean that confirming that relationship is ethical. And nothing good can come from engaging publicly with someone who was unhappy with your services—it is only going to make you look bad.

For that happy client who tagged you, it's appropriate for you to send them a secure message or email thanking them for the tag, and, if you're available, asking them to post your website or contact information. This leaves all disclosures in your client's hands and prevents you from acting in a way that may violate HIPAA or leave you in ethically dubious waters. You could also just post "thanks for the tag" and post your website yourself, without specifically confirming your relationship.

Some lactation consultants are interested in running Facebook groups for their clients to facilitate parent-to-parent support, and this offering may be very appealing to families as a client perk. However, you must be very, very clear with your clients about the privacy pitfalls of a Facebook group, and obtain explicit consent that specifies that once they join the group, you are unable to protect their privacy with respect to their clinical care. As above, remind your clients that you will not give them specific clinical recommendations in the group. Rather, the group is for families to connect and support each other.

If you do run such a group, be mindful that you will need to stay on top of all the conversations that take place. And that can be a lot of work and take precious time away from your clients, your business, and your family. A common group issue arises when one member establishes themselves as an expert on a topic, and begins to offer what can be considered clinical or sometimes even legal advice. This can be a liability for you, as group members may believe that you endorse and support all opinions posted on the page. A disclaimer is critical, and I have sample disclaimers available in my store. Additionally, you can change your group settings so that you have to approve all members and posts and all comments before they are published. This way, you can get ahead of any potential problems. Your group should be a "secret" group to offer the most privacy protection possible on Facebook.

A big challenge of running a Facebook group is coping with the inevitable conflicts that arise. Having clear posting policies, including topics that are off-limits, can be helpful. But what do you do when group members start attacking one another? You'll need to dig deep into your communications skills to defuse the conflict in a way that shows respect to all parties. If the group is composed of your clients, a good idea might be to take the post down, and call each person directly to give them a safe space to share their feelings and frustrations. Nipping potentially contentious conversations in the bud requires vigilance.

It is not recommended that you allow group members to be admins on your group unless you are willing to take full responsibility for everything they post or do in the group. Any group admin you have becomes a proxy, or stand-in, for you, and you need to have full confidence that they will act appropriately on your behalf. Even though you've made it clear to your group members that you cannot protect them under HIPAA if they join your group, it's still risky to allow a non-covered entity to have administrative control of your group. You just never know what may happen.

If you work with interns or have CLCs working under you, presumably they have signed a Business Associate's Agreement with you, and they may be an ideal person to run a group for you. You could provide appropriate oversight within the context of the mentorship agreement or terms of employment, and offer them an opportunity to develop their communications skills.

There are a plethora of Facebook groups for those of us working in lactation or aspiring to become IBCLCs. They can be immensely valuable resources for brainstorming tricky situations, learning about educational opportunities, and getting emotional support from people who understand what it's like to be an IBCLC.

If you've spent any amount of time on social media, especially in Facebook groups or on Twitter, you know that emotions can run high and it can be easy to lose your cool. This can be detrimental to your professional image, and it's crucial that you practice mindfulness, discretion, and intention in all of your online relationships and interactions. Here are some general principles to keep in mind:

- Obtain explicit permission before posting about a client
- Obtain explicit permission before sharing any client photos

- Even with permission, do not share any PHI
- Be professional in your tone and interactions within the group
- Check the specific posting guidelines for each group and follow them
- Stick to professional, not personal topics
- Assume positive intent when reading a post or comment
- Before commenting, ask yourself if you are adding value to the conversation in a spirit of collaboration and collegiality
- Keep interpersonal conflicts private when possible. If you have an issue with another group member, start with the group admins to resolve the conflict in a way that promotes peace

Social media platforms are engineered to make you want to visit frequently by rewarding you when you post or share something of your own, or like or comment on something posted or shared by someone else. The algorithms use our behaviors to help advertisers reach us in a frighteningly targeted way (how many of us lactation consultants see ads for bras in our Facebook feed?), and to create within us an emotional need for the validation of others so that we will be compelled to contribute. Without us, there would be no content on any social media. In traditional media, the producer makes the content and the audience receives it. In social media, the content is both generated and received by the audience.

I bring this up because we are all vulnerable to the potentially harmful effects of social media. Even though social media can be a useful tool for business promotion and professional development, you need to know what you can handle. For some of you, participation in social media may be emotionally unhealthy or even risky for you. I urge you to put your own wellness above any business or professional goals you may have.

Furthermore, we may be in a unique position to identify red flags for perinatal mood disorders like postpartum depression or postpartum anxiety by observing the ways in which our clients use social media. For example, if you are in a parent group, you may see your client post something related to their breastfeeding issues that makes you feel concerned about their emotional state. It would be completely inappropriate to comment on that thread, but you could certainly reach out to them to mention you saw what they posted, and gently offer your concerns and resources focused on their postpartum wellness.

Social Media Ethics:

- Social Media Disclaimers, Permission to Post, Photo Consent, and Email Scripts
- Legal and Ethical Issues for the IBCLC by Elizabeth Brooks, JD, IBCLC
- Thin Ice Ahead! Offering Lactation Help on Social Media and Cell Phones
- Insta-gram or Insta-gasp? The Ethics of Sharing on Social Media for Birth Professionals
- What's Too "Friendly" for an IBCLC on Social Media?
- Social Media and Health Care Professionals: Benefits, Risks, and Best Practices
- Social Media Policy (for Therapists)

Social Media How-Tos:

- What's Really the Difference Between Facebook Pages, Groups and Profiles?
- Facebook Groups Vs Pages: The Definitive Guide
- Facebook Page vs Group: A Facebook Marketing Dilemma
- The 15 Rules of Facebook Group Engagement

Social Media Pitfalls:

- Threaten My Group, and I'll Belittle Your Science
- Civility in the Digital Age: How Companies and People Can Triumph over Haters, Trolls, Bullies and Other Jerks by Andrea Weckerle
- Biological & Psychological Reasons for Social Media Addiction
- How Your Biased Brain Makes You a Jerk Online (and How to Stop It) (contains adult language)
- 6 Scientific Reasons Facebook Turns Everybody Into A Jerk (contains adult language)

Facebook groups for lactation professionals:

- Paperless Private Practice for the IBCLC – this is my group
- BFN – IBCLCs in PP
- PP IBCLC
- IBCLCs in Private Practice
- IBCLC Credential Protection and Promotion
- IBCLCs in Network with Aetna
- Paperless IBCLC
- Want to be an IBCLC?
- African-American IBCLCs
- Canadian IBCLCs
- ICAP (International Consortium of Ankylofrenula Professionals)
- BFN – Tongue Tie Professionals
- GOLD Lactation Conference Discussion
- LCinPP (only for those who have attended the conference at least once)

RUNNING YOUR IBCLC PRIVATE PRACTICE

Time to get down to the nitty-gritty. In this chapter, I will take you step-by-step through working with a client from the moment of first contact through "graduating" them from your services. I'll also cover some common IBCLC-client conflicts and offer coping strategies and ideas for effective conflict-resolution strategies.

Note: many IBCLCs have adopted the use of Electronic Health Record (EHR) platforms for client management and charting. If you are curious to learn more about what's out there, check out my website where I have continuously updated resources on EHR platforms, including comparisons, reviews, and trainings.

Typical IBCLC Client Workflow

Initial Outreach

It all starts with a phone call, or a text, or an email, or a direct message on social media, or bat-signal if you've integrated that technology into your private practice.

Someone needs help!

Nipple pain, engorged breasts, non-latching babies, formula supplementation, a scary pediatrician visit—families are often reaching out to us at very low moments in their lives. From the very outset, we are privy to their intimate fears and worries, and they are vulnerable because they are hoping we will change their situation for the better.

Seemingly small breastfeeding challenges can escalate so rapidly that it's important to see clients as soon as possible, usually within 48 hours. If you don't have any open appointments within an appropriate time frame, refer the family to another IBCLC. Even though it may feel like giving business away, if you're referring to colleagues with whom you have a collegial relationship, these referrals will come back around your way when those other IBCLCs are booked or on vacation. Referring out can become a mutually beneficial relationship for you and your colleague. Helping families to get help quickly is good for overall breastfeeding outcomes in your community, which in turn will increase demand for IBCLC services. For those of you in communities or areas without enough IBCLCs, you may not have anyone to refer to when you get busy, and this particular problem just doesn't have an easy answer. I encourage you to reach out for online support from other IBCLCs to help you with the emotional aspects, which can include loneliness and frustration.

Often, you'll get an appointment request that includes lots of specific details and requests for help. Remember—they are not yet your client, but by offering any information or advice you may be creating a client relationship without the protection of a consent for care. Offering general information or links to evidence-base resources can be helpful in tiding them over until they can see you or a colleague, as long as you make it clear that you are not speaking into their specific situation. You can also refer them to free resources like La Leche League or Breastfeeding USA, and/or to appropriate medical professionals like a pediatrician, midwife, obstetrician, mental health provider, tongue tie specialists, and others.

If you do home visits, you'll need to confirm that the family is in your service area. A potential client may be in your service area, and you may have an open appointment, but if you'll have to travel from one end of your service area to another, you may not have enough time to see both of them. This happens with me all the time. If I am booked to see a client in Sunset Park, at the southern edge of Brooklyn, and I get an appointment request from a client in Kew Gardens in central Queens, that journey could take me more than an hour, and a hard hour at that, mostly spent sitting in bumper-to-bumper traffic. I just can't do it. I have to be intentional about grouping my clients geographically so I don't burn out.

If you're available, it's time to schedule the appointment, and I'll take you through that in the next section.

Scheduling

In order to schedule an appointment with a client, they'll need some information from you. You'll tell them the day and time you have available (or multiple options if possible), and share your payment and cancellation policies. If you are in-network with their insurance provider, you'll need to see a copy of their card so that you can confirm their benefits.

Once the client has agreed to your payment policies or provided their insurance card, and if the schedule works for both of you, put them in your calendar and send them confirmation of their appointment. Some IBCLCs will take payment at the time that the appointment is booked. If you have a cancellation policy, communicate that very clearly.

Next, you'll want to tell your client how to prepare for your visit. I ask them to complete my intake (which is online). I tell them what information I will want, such as record of weights, feeding and diaper logs, and I'll invite them to use online scheduling.

You can schedule visits directly with your clients using phone, text, or email. Interactions with potential clients are not subject to HIPAA provisions, because you do not have a relationship with them. But be careful not to start offering clinical recommendations in the course of booking the appointment. Once the appointment is scheduled, HIPAA takes effect.

Online scheduling allows clients to book with you through your website or a third-party system. Many EHR platforms include online scheduling as a built-in feature, and there are also standalone schedulers that are HIPAA compliant. See my website for continually updated reviews and recommendations.

Intake

Intake refers to the process by which a client's chart is created. Some IBCLCs like to have clients complete an intake in advance, and most EHR platforms include this functionality. If you're interested in using an EHR to do the intake in advance, please see my other book *Paperless Private Practice for Lactation Consultants* and my website for education and instruction on this topic. You can also do the intake in person.

Before you start taking the history that provides the underpinnings of the chart, you'll want your client to sign your legal forms. Once they have signed those forms, they are officially your client, and you can begin your journey together.

- Paperless Private Practice for the IBCLC
- Informed Consent: Ethical Obligation or Legal Compulsion?

History-Taking and Documentation

As previously discussed, you'll be taking a written record of everything that occurs during the visit. You can do this freestyle, or you can use a purchased template or an EHR platform, which will include charting templates, either pre-installed or customizable.

If you have purchased charting templates from anyone (including those included in my published resources), or if your EHR platform comes with charting templates, be mindful that these templates reflect the styles, degree of lactation education, and biases of the creators. Before implementing them in your practice, look carefully at your purchased templates and ask yourself what changes and modifications you need to make so that you can include every detail that's important to you. Remember that any tool must be an extension of your brain, and without customization you're just letting someone else do the thinking for you.

At all times, maintain a judgement-free demeanor when talking with your clients. Families take all sorts of paths in the journey of parenthood, and the medical interventions can be enlightening to us as we work towards helping our clients solve and overcome their breastfeeding challenges. Often we are privileged to become safe spaces for our clients to share fears and concerns that other healthcare providers may not ask about, and we can make this happen by meeting our clients where they are and offering them acceptance and support.

Charting is an essential part of informed consent, where you document which procedures or interventions were offered or recommended, along clinical indications, risks and benefits, alternatives, referrals for specialists or second opinions, and next steps for follow-up. Your client is free to accept or reject any procedure or intervention, but it is essential that you provide a complete picture and document everything.

Charting:

- How to keep good clinical records
- History and Assessment: It's All in the Details by Denise Altman
- Breastfeeding and Human Lactation
- EHR Comparison Chart
- Diana West's Clinical Forms
- G-Suite for IBCLCs
- Milk Notes
- Mobile Lactation Consultant
- Top 10 Tips for Effective Use of EHRs
- 9 Tips for Writing Rock-Solid Medical Charts

Informed Consent:

- Avoiding Malpractice Through Strong Informed Consent Practices
- The 5 Elements of Informed Consent

- Informed Consent: A Process of Communication

Client History

The first written piece of your client's chart will be their history. This is where you gather all the relevant information necessary to understand where your client and their baby are coming from.

Base Client Information

Up front, you will want key information available at a glance as soon as you open your client's chart. Client's name and date of birth, baby's name, baby's date of birth, and baby's birth weight are the primary fields you will want in this section.

Contact Information

Contact information includes not only name and address, but also insurance information (if you take insurance), emergency contacts (like the parent's partner or other primary support person), and information on other members of the healthcare team such as the baby's pediatrician and the parent's obstetrician/midwife.

Demographic Information

Demographic information is typically understood to be any data that could be used for marketing purposes, such as sex, income, or age. For the purposes of IBCLC private practice, it is useful to collect the client's birth date, occupation, partner's name and occupation (if the client is partnered), any other languages spoken in the home, and any relevant cultural or religious practices they want me to know about in advance.

I work in an extremely ethnically diverse setting (Queens, NY) and am often working with immigrants or the children of immigrants. I do not ask my clients about their ethnic backgrounds or where they are from. These are loaded questions that imply that they do not belong. However, if I hear them speaking a language other than English, I will ask what language they are speaking. That often opens up an enjoyable conversation about culture and heritage that takes place on the client's terms.

In terms of cultural or religious practices, some may impact the course of the lactation visit. For example, some groups wait to name their babies until a special ceremony; if you are seeing the family before that ceremony, they will not tell you the baby's name. When in doubt, ask—but make sure you ask in a non-exclusionary way. "What would you like me to know about this?" is an open question that put the client in control of the direction of the conversation. In contrast, asking a client if they perform a certain specific practice positions you as an authority on their culture and now the conversation is happening on your terms, not theirs, and that is a trust-killer.

If your client or their partner is not cisgender, use the pronoun that they prefer. Asking, "how would you like me to refer to you?" demonstrates respect and removes your (explicit or inadvertent) biases from the conversation.

- <u>Cultural Competence or Cultural Humility? A Roadmap for Lactation Specialists</u>
- <u>The Importance of Cultural Diversity in Healthcare</u>
- <u>Cultural Competence in Breastfeeding Promotion</u>
- <u>A Guide to Culturally Competent Nursing Care</u>
- <u>Words that Hurt</u> (trigger warning—contains, vulgar, offensive, bigoted, and explicit language to explain why certain words and phrases are problematic)

Social History

The social history is where we inquire into personal aspects of our client's lifestyles—and it is often where we obtain information critical to providing effective care. In this section of the history, you will ask your client about use of tobacco, caffeine, recreational drugs, illicit drugs, and alcohol.

You may also want to ask your client if they are enrolled in any public programs, such as WIC (Women, Infants, and Children) in the US, and if they have any concerns about their ability to provide financially for their babies or themselves. You can also ask if they have a history of abuse and if they are currently being abused or feel unsafe.

Do not assume your clients are married, heterosexual, or in a relationship. Ask them if they have a primary support person, and to identify their relationship with that person. Then, find out who else is in their support network, and whether or not those people are supportive of breastfeeding.

Ask if your clients are planning to return to work, and gather information about their work setting and childcare plans. This is a good place to find out if your client will need a breast pump and if they have obtained one already.

Find out what your client's goals are for breastfeeding so that you can tailor your care appropriately. Understand that this is their journey and the stated goals may not conform to outside standards for breastfeeding duration. It is your job to hear your client and meet them where they are, knowing that when breastfeeding is well established, many parents find themselves meeting or even exceeding their own stated goals.

- What Should Go in a Social History?
- Rethinking the Social History
- Social History is Part of Medical History
- The Social History Matters!

Health History

Within this section, you'll collect information on your client's *past* health information. You're not asking about what's going on at present, but finding out what may be contributing to the present situation. You will be gathering data not only on your client, but on their baby, and on immediate family members. In your training and education to qualify for the IBLCE exam you will have learned what health and medical conditions can have an impact on breastfeeding; please refer to lactation textbooks and courses in order to develop the components of an effective history. Here is a list of common sections in the health history to get you started:

- Health conditions, disorders, and chronic illnesses for client and immediate family
- Surgical history (specifically related to the breast)
- Thyroid history
- Fertility history
- Previous lactation history
- Medications, herbs, and supplement with dosage amounts
- Allergies, intolerances, and sensitivities, as well as dietary preferences or limitations
- History of psychiatric conditions or mood disorders

Pay particular attention to disorders, illnesses, and conditions that affect the endocrinal system, as well as any history of cancer of the breast, thyroid, or pituitary. Ask about hormonal imbalances and conditions such as polycystic ovarian syndrome, and about use of hormonal contraceptives in the past. Document any assisted reproductive technologies used by the client, and any hormonal treatments undertaken and reason for seeking those treatments.

Ask your clients about life choices they make with regard to their health. Your clients may be avoiding certain foods or following a specific diet because of chronic or current health concerns. Make sure to ask lots of questions about any autoimmune disorders in the client's history, such as eczema, allergies, and gastrointestinal diseases and conditions. Learn about their overall health before becoming pregnant, and ask if anything has changed.

If they have diabetes, hypertension, heart disease, or cancer, or a family history of any of those diseases, you'll want to know.

This may seem like a lot of detail, but any experienced IBCLC will tell you that breastfeeding is so complicated that you really can't learn too much about your clients. We are dealing with a biological process that can be impacted by so many factors, and often we are the only ones putting the pieces together. People generally like to talk about themselves, and keeping this portion of the history friendly and conversational can help.

If you use an EHR platform, it may include a Review of Systems, which documents illnesses, complaints, or chronic conditions within the major organ systems that are separate from the client's current problem. Performing an ROS may be outside of your scope of practice; however, asking your clients about their overall health may uncover issues that they have not brought up with their primary care providers. Refer your clients to a doctor or midwife if they have any unaddressed health concerns that are outside of your scope of practice.

- Adult Review of Systems (ROS)
- How Does Review of Systems Differ from History of Present Illness?
- Collecting Health History Information

Pregnancy, Labor, and Delivery

Once you've gone over general health information, you're going to delve into the client's pregnancy, labor, and delivery history with this baby (or babies, if you're working with twins or higher order multiples).

You'll want to know absolutely everything, so take your time here. Your client should share any conditions they dealt with during pregnancy, and you will want to ask about stress levels and exercise during pregnancy. Ask about breast changes during pregnancy and postpartum, and if they expressed colostrum prenatally.

Have your clients share their birth stories from the beginning. During this part of the consult, you may want to set your clipboard or tablet aside to give your client your full attention. They are sharing an unparalleled event in their lives, one that may have rocked their foundations and altered their perception of themselves. The key data points you will need to collect about the labor include:

- Location of labor and birth (hospital, freestanding birth center, home, car)
- Duration of labor
- Duration of pushing stage
- Pain management
- Interventions to induce or augment labor
- Medication to induce or augment labor
- Interventions during the labor and the birth
- Type of birth
- Postpartum complications

At this point, you may want to ask your client how they are presently feeling, and share with them the post-birth warning symptoms. If they have any of these warning symptoms, have them call their doctor or midwife immediately. You can also screen for perinatal mood disorders here, especially if they have shared that their birth was upsetting or traumatic.

- Impact of Birthing Practices on Breastfeeding by Linda J. Smith
- Learn These Post-Birth Warning Signs
- Professional Tools from Postpartum Support International
- What is Birth Trauma?

Infant Information

Finally, it's time to learn all about the baby or babies. You'll need:

- Baby's name
- Baby's sex
- Baby's date of birth
- Birth weight
- Date of discharge
- Discharge weight
- Most recent weight
- Interventions during and after birth
- NICU details, if applicable
- Any health issues or concerns for the baby
- Any medications the baby is using
- Any allergies the baby has
- If metabolic disorder was detected during screening

Be sure to ask about suctioning, because in my experience even though my intake mentions suctioning, many clients forget to mention it when completing my online forms so I always ask twice.

Find out how breastfeeding has been going. Have your clients start with the very first moments after birth, and ask if the baby latched right away. If the baby spent time in the NICU, ask what devices were used for feeding the baby. When supplementation has occurred, document what supplement was used and how it was delivered.

Before completing the history and moving into the encounter itself, ask your client what else they would like you to know that you didn't ask. Giving your clients this space can yield enlightening results and also works to build trust.

Charting Encounters

Every time you connect with a client, whether it is in person, by phone, or through any other communication method, this is considered an "encounter" and you must document it in your client's chart. So what are you supposed to include?

You can document these encounters any way you like, but I recommend incorporating a format known as a SOAP note into your workflow. SOAP, an acronym which stands for Subjective, Objective, Assessment, and Plan, is commonly used across medical and health disciplines as a way to organize the client's chart.

When should you chart? The further away you are from the visit, the more likely it is that you will forget important details, get things wrong, or fail to do it altogether. Including charting within the visit itself is going to be the best way to insure that it happens.

If you are making sure that your clients are getting lots of eye contact and attention when it matters—when they tell the birth story, when they describe how breastfeeding is going, when they share with you their fears and their worries and all those big emotions—then it's not likely to bother them that you are writing down her answers when you are asking her questions about diaper count and feeding and other factual information.

Tell your families what you're doing. Say, "I'm just going to take a moment to write all this down. It's important to me that I don't lose track of anything you are saying." Or, "This is such good information. Give me a sec to get it all own." Or, "I'm going to work on your care plan. While I'm writing, please think of questions you have for me while I'm still here." This is client-centered charting, but doesn't ignore your very real need to make time for the administrative aspects of your work.

Your chart is not complete until you have signed it, and once you've signed it you should not make any alterations. If you're using an EHR platform, the sign feature will be built in and often will lock charts to edits. Use of an EHR will produce an electronic trail that will be useful if you are audited by an insurance company or (eek) sued by a client. Paper files should also be signed, and you will want to have a way to document when charts are accessed. A list on the front of the folder noting who accessed the chart and the date and time along with a signature may meet these requirements.

- <u>SOAP Notes</u>
- <u>SOAP Notes: Getting Down and Dirty with Medical Translation</u>
- <u>How to Take Clinical Notes Using SOAP</u>
- <u>SOAP Notes Sections</u>
- <u>Privacy and Security Audits of Electronic Health Information</u>
- <u>How to Stay HIPAA Compliant with Audit Logs</u>

Subjective

In the subjective portion of your chart, you will be asking your clients lots of questions about what has been going on with the client, the client's baby, and breastfeeding. The client will be sharing their experience, their feelings, and their own observations. You will not be adding commentary, analysis, or interpretation, simply recording what your client wants you to know and the information you need to start putting the pieces together. This includes:

- Issues the client is dealing with
- Feeding, supplementing, diaper, and pumping logs for the previous 24-48 hours
- Descriptions of what feedings are like
- Descriptions of the baby's behavior
- Descriptions of the mother's experience

As much as possible, combine open-ended questions like "What are you most concerned about?" with closed questions like "How many wet diapers has your baby had since this time yesterday?"

This a time for your client to share their experience, be heard by someone who cares, receive emotional validation. Resist the urge to rush just to check off boxes on your charting form, because your client may have to tap into painful or scary feelings in order to give you the information you need.

Often, some of these subjective elements come out when you are taking the history, so having a charting system that allows you to move back and forth between those sections will be helpful.

- Breastfeeding Answers Made Simple by Nancy Mohrbacher
- Communications Skills: Listening and Learning
- Creating Connection: Communication Skills for Lactation Educators
- Mothers Speak Out: Top Five Traits of a Great Lactation Consultant
- When Tears Flow and Milk Doesn't: Support Through Breastfeeding Grief
- Healing Breastfeeding Grief: How mothers feel and heal when breastfeeding does not go as hoped by Hilary Jacobson

Objective

In the Objective section of the SOAP note, you'll be recording everything you observe about the parent and their baby or babies as you work with them. The tools you will use are often called assessment tools, so it's helpful to remember that the Objective section and the Assessment section are actually the two components of your clinical interpretation of everything that's going on with the family. Here, you'll gather data, and in the next section you'll interpret your findings.

Because you are working with two people (or more, with multiples), you'll need to perform observations of both the parent and the baby, as well as observations of a shared activity by looking at what happens during a feeding. Stick to what you can determine with your senses ("scale showed transfer of 48mls), and refrain from using qualifying or subjective language ("baby had a good feed").

Let's take a closer look at the kinds of information you'll need. In the maternal section, you'll be looking at the breast and nipple anatomy, recording data about the type of milk (from colostrum through transitional to mature milk) and when secretory activation (sometimes called lactogenesis II) occurred. Some IBCLCs use breast diagrams in order to indicate the location of palpable plugged ducts, to draw the shape and orientation of cracks and fissures on the nipples, or to shade in an area that may be reddened or warm. A diagram can also be useful for drawing axillary breast tissue or showing the location of any prior surgical scars.

The infant assessment should be as comprehensive as your training allows. I recommend seeking out as much training as possible on oral anatomy and biomechanics, the musculoskeletal system, how to identify structural abnormalities or asymmetries that can affect breastfeeding, and normal and atypical infant behavior relative to age. You will want to be up-to-date on validated assessment tools used in the field, particularly if you are going to be referring an infant for a treatment like a frenotomy. It is outside the scope of this book to teach you how to choose and use assessment tools or how to perform an infant observation, but in the resources section I will provide some direction for you to gain the skills and education you need. Working with a seasoned IBCLC mentor is a great option for strengthening your skills, even if you are already an IBCLC.

When you observe a feeding, you will be recording information about how the parent and baby are working together. You may be recording the baby's weight before and after a feeding, and as long as you are using the right scale (see the section on Physical Supplies), this can be a useful data point. But remember, a test weigh is only a snapshot—it tells you what happened this time, not what is happening overall. You want to write down what you are seeing and hearing when baby sucks and swallows (or doesn't), and describe how the feeding ends. Ask about the mother's levels of pain, and whether they change or vary during the feeding. Record the length of the feeding, and which side was used. If the parent used a nipple shield, at-breast supplementer, or other device, indicate that as well. Sometimes the parent will provide their own subjective statements during a feeding, and it's appropriate to record those as quotes from the parent.

- History and Assessment: It's All In the Details by Denise Altman
- The Breastfeeding Atlas by Barbara Wilson-Clay and Kay Hoover
- Looking Closely at the Baby
- Breast Assessment: What, Why, How, and When
- Diagnosis and Management of Tongue Tie and Lip Tie in Breastfeeding
- Neuromusculoskeletal disorders in the breastfed baby: causes, assessment, & treatment
- Organization of tongue movements before and after frenotomy for posterior tongue-tie: an Ultrasound analysis
- Structure and Function: Causes and Possible Long Term Consequences

Assessment

As you listen to the parent's subjective experience and record objective information, you will begin to formulate your theories about the situation, and you'll write these in the Assessment area. You are not diagnosing a condition, you are offering a possible interpretation, so use words like "possible" or "suspected" to qualify your statements so you're not acting outside your scope of practice.

Be as detailed as possible, backing up your theories with your observations. You may or may not intend for your clients to read this section; you will likely want their pediatrician or other healthcare provider to see it. Be mindful that your clients can request access to their charts at any point, so word appropriately.

- GOLD Learning YouTube Channel
- Counseling the Nursing Mother: A Lactation Consultant's Guide
- Every Patient Tells a Story: Medical Mysteries and the Art of Diagnosis
- Case Studies in Breastfeeding: Problem-Solving Skills and Strategies

Plan

The Plan section is where you will provide your client with instructions for managing their current situation, referrals to other care providers, and an explanation for how follow-up will work. Each care plan will be unique to every family you see; however, you'll want to make sure your protocols are backed by the latest research and information available. There is never going to be a one-size-fits-all solution for your clients and their babies, and a personalized plan may be more likely to be implemented.

You'll want to write this section using everyday language as free from clinical jargon as possible. Provide your clients with concrete steps ("pump 8x/day with a hospital-grade pump") and not vague recommendations ("get your milk supply up"). Research the best internet-based resources for parents specific to every situation, and provide those in your care plan. Remember that you're dealing with people who worried, anxious, stressed, and sleep-deprived, and aren't necessarily up for the task of filling in the blanks. Give them clear markers for self-assessment.

The Plan section will also be shared with the pediatrician and can be a great tool for advocacy. When I curate links to share with my clients, I focus on resources that are published on websites that are overseen by an IBCLC or MD, or are written by IBCLCs who also provide continuing education and/or have written books in the field. I never link to blogs by parents, message board posts, or articles on content aggregators (such as Huffington Post). Periodically, I review my resources to make sure they are up to date and that no links are broken.

There are differences of opinion about what should go to the pediatrician. A brief report may be more likely to be read by a busy physician. On the other hand, you never know if something you say may lead a pediatrician to make positive changes in their own practice. The bigger picture is that we need to ask ourselves if our practices will contribute to improved health outcomes. If you are going to include lots of information, make sure it's formatted in a way that highlights what's important for the pediatrician to see. At the very least, a pediatrician report is another form of documentation in the case of client non-compliance with your care plan.

- Journal of Human Lactation
- Clinical Lactation (USLCA publication)
- Clinics in Human Lactation (Monograph Series)
- Academy of Breastfeeding Medicine Protocols
- Managing Challenges at the Breast Lecture Pack
- Selecting and Using Breastfeeding Tools: Improving Care and Outcomes by Catherine Watson Genna
- Supporting Sucking Skills in Breastfeeding Infants by Catherine Watson Genna
- Finding Sufficiency: Breastfeeding With Insufficient Glandular Tissue by Diana Cassar-Uhl
- The Breastfeeding Mother's Guide to Making More Milk by Diana West (a new edition is forthcoming)

- Defining Your Own Success: Breastfeeding After Breast Reduction Surgery by Diana West
- Breastfeeding Without Birthing: A Breastfeeding Guide for Mothers through Adoption, Surrogacy, and Other Special Circumstances by Alyssa Schnell
- New Thoughts on Infant Pre and Post-Frenotomy Care
- TummyTime!™ : A Therapeutic Strategy for Parents and Babies
- Why Bodywork is a Significant Piece of the Puzzle of Comprehensive Tongue & Lip Tie Treatment? — The Emerging GOLD Standard of Treatment & Care

Other Chart Data

Your client's chart will need to include the diagnosis and procedure (CPT) codes, which I discuss in detail in the chapter on billing. Include the location where the visit took place, the start time, the duration, and any other people present. If others are present, specify that client gave explicit consent for them to sit in. If you have a follow-up scheduled, indicate that on the chart.

Other Types of Encounters

When you speak with a client on the phone or exchange a round of text or email messages (with all privacy protections in place), you must add a record of this to their chart. You don't necessarily need to provide full SOAP format; a brief summary is often all that is required. Basically, the goal is to document any changes or updates to the client's current issue(s) and any modifications to the care plan.

- Breastfeeding Answers Made Simple: A Pocket Guide for Helping Mothers by Nancy Mohrbacher
- Brief Breastfeeding Encounters: Effective Counseling Techniques When Time is Limited

- <u>Does telephone lactation counselling improve breastfeeding practices? A randomised controlled trial</u>
- <u>Telephone Peer Counseling of Breastfeeding Among WIC Participants: A Randomized Controlled Trial</u>

Payments and Billing

During the visit, you will be collecting payment from your self-pay clients, and providing them with a superbill as a receipt. For your insurance clients, you'll be generating the codes you or your biller needs to create the CMS-1500 that will be submitted so you can be paid. Document all charges, claims, and payments in your client's chart as well as through your own bookkeeping system.

You must charge your clients consistently, but you are free to offer discounts at your discretion. When giving a client a discount, you still must charge them the full amount, then reflect the discount on the superbill by showing that the amount paid was less. See the section on Fee For Service for more information.

Sending Reports

Sending reports encompasses both sending the care plan to the client, and sending a clinical report to their healthcare provider.

The client care plan should be simple; just the information in the Plan section of the SOAP note (along with the baby's weight) is generally sufficient. Your client has the right to request access to their full chart at any time, but most postpartum families do not want that level of data.

For reports sent to the pediatrician, an abbreviated version of the SOAP note usually suffices. You are not sending everything the client told you or everything you observed, but rather a summary of the Subjective reportings and Objective findings, along with the full Assessment and Plan. Attaching a copy of any assessment tools used can bolster your recommendations.

These reports can be sent through secure messaging or email (with HIPAA provisions in place), or by fax. There are many services out there that offer email-to-fax, where you use your computer to generate a PDF, and the service turns it into a fax. I have more on this in *Paperless Private Practice for Lactation Consultants.* You can always leave behind a hard copy of the care plan, if you're old-school and have paper assessments on carbon triplicate paper, and mail a copy to the pediatrician. Whatever the delivery method, you need to send these reports to comply with the IBLCE Code of Professional Conduct.

- Sending Reports: What's in it for IBCLCs?
- Increasing Your Credibility with Physicians: Strategies for Lactation Consultants
- The SHARE Approach: A Model for Shared Decisionmaking - Fact Sheet
- What is Allied Health?
- Frees, Robin B. "Don't Wait: Make Yourself A Part of the Healthcare Team." ILCA 2001. This article is behind a paywall with no direct link available but is highly worth reading.

Follow-Up

When you set your payment policies, you determined what limits (if any) you placed on following up with your client. Most IBCLCs are including some degree of follow-up in the fees for their services, usually support through phone, text, and email and a discount on a follow-up visit. This is all communicated to your client through your Payment Policies and recorded in your Policies and Procedures manual.

Some of you may feel apprehensive about suggesting that self-pay clients book an in-person follow-up. After all, they have already paid so much money to you and insurance reimbursement is uncertain. What will they think if you ask them to pay for another visit? But think of it this way—these families have hired an expert in breastfeeding. And as an expert, you know that as the care plan is implemented, the situation is going to change, sometimes dramatically, and there is only so much you can do to troubleshoot and optimize over email. Suggesting to these families that an in-person follow-up to assess progress and update the care plan can make a big difference in their ability to achieve their breastfeeding goals. Be confident in this recommendation. You're not a kid asking for a raise in your allowance. You're a professional breastfeeding expert who knows that ongoing support is better than a bandaid and some well wishes.

I've modified my follow-up policies several times over the years. Currently, I tell my self-pay clients that I can provide 2 weeks of email and text (with appropriate protections in place), but after that they have to see me again in person if they still need help with the current problem or if a new problem arises. I also tell them that I am always going to be available to them as a cheerleader and that baby pictures make my day.

I like to check in with my clients after a few days if I don't hear from them first. When they text me, if it's short and positive I'll text back an affirmation. If the text is lengthy and full of questions, I reply that I'll be writing them an email, and I wait until later so I can sit down and be intentional about my reply.

We all have clients who blow up our inboxes with question after question, and their urgency can trigger our caregiving urge to "tend and befriend." Before you stop what you are doing to engage with a distraught client over text, stop and evaluate the content of the message. Where is the urgency? Is it in the situation itself, or is it in your client's feelings about the situation?

If the urgency is in the situation itself, next consider whether this urgent situation requires immediate action. And by immediate, I mean, "right this second." There are some cases where you'll need to recommend she see a medical doctor or go to her nearest emergency room. When this happens, such as a client with a high fever and reddened area on her breast, or a baby who is showing signs of dehydration, the family must get the appropriate medical interventions before breastfeeding can be addressed.

If the client is texting you about something that is not medically urgent or emergent, but still clinically troublesome, refrain from trying to solve this problem over text or even email. For example, a client will say that they had a bad visit with the pediatrician and the baby didn't gain enough weight. Ask the client to tell you the baby's weight, and say that you will email her later when you've had a chance to pull up her chart. When responding to these issues, refer your client back to the care plan, offer resources for self-efficacy, and recommend a follow-up visit with you.

Your client will respond along a spectrum that runs between scheduling that in-person visit to expressing emotional responses that may seem to be clouding their ability to interpret or act on the care plan. It is never going to be wrong to suggest to any of your clients that breastfeeding troubles and postpartum depression and anxiety can go hand in hand, and to reach out sooner rather than later. For those clients who just keep texting and texting and texting, use emotional validation ("You are so worried about weight gain"), express your own emotions ("I'm concerned because you're showing some red flags for postpartum anxiety") and offer the appropriate resource ("Please share these feelings with your care provider and I'm happy to provide you with therapist recommendations").

In a small percentage of cases you may feel worried that the family isn't going to act appropriately on a pressing concern, such as when a baby is slow to gain but the family is prioritizing sleep. Please don't keep those concerns to yourself; include them in the care plan and follow up with a call to the pediatrician. The pediatrician can also assess and refer for perinatal mood disorders.

- <u>What Happens Next? Customizable Handout for IBCLCs</u>

- Perinatal Mental Health: Research and Practical Applications Lecture Pack
- Postpartum Support International
- Postpartum Depression Facts
- The Hidden Feelings of Motherhood Second Edition by Kathleen A. Kendall-Tackett
- Healing Breastfeeding Grief: How mothers feel and heal when breastfeeding does not go as hoped by Hilary Jacobson
- Legal and Ethical Issues for the IBCLC by Elizabeth Brooks
- Depression and anxiety during the perinatal period

Release of Client

If you want to formally end the client relationship after the follow-up period concludes, you can send them a brief note releasing them from your care. If applicable, you can also use this note to invite them to continue the relationship by booking another in-person appointment. You may also want to send them a client satisfaction survey to gather feedback (both positive and negative) towards improving your practices.

- Annie Frisbie's Charting Templates (includes client release form and satisfaction survey)
- Measuring Patient Satisfaction: How to Do It and Why to Bother
- The Patient Satisfaction Survey: A Diagnostic Tool

Record Storage

Your clients have the right to ask for their chart. Check with your state for laws regarding record storage, as there are no federal guidelines in place. In most places records must be kept until at least the age of majority. Storage should be locked and secure.

- Does the HIPAA Privacy Rule require covered entities to keep patients' medical records for any period of time?
- Pointers for psychologists on client record retention
- Record Retention: How Long? And What Should be Kept After the Deadline?

Other Kinds of Lactation Visits

Prenatal Visits

Families may contact you before their baby arrives for a prenatal consult, which you can offer one-on-one or in a group setting. Familiarity with birth culture in your area will help you tailor your information towards what your clients can expect in the hospital and how you can help them once they return home. Your clients may ask you for recommendations for doulas and childbirth classes (but remember that these recommendations should never involve any kickbacks).

It may be tempting to structure your class around the perfect initiation of breastfeeding—skin to skin for 90 minutes after an unmedicated birth, with all neonatal procedures and tests delayed until after the first latch, and full-time rooming-in during the hospital stay. However, our clients are birthing in the real world, and it may be more useful for them to have strategies for coping with common hospital-based challenges, such as:

- Breastfeeding is not initiated immediately
- Baby is not latching
- Baby is sleepy from birth interventions
- Baby receives suctioning or has a nasogastric tube in the NICU

- Mother is recovering from surgical birth
- Mother is told she has flat nipples
- Mother has pain during latch

Providing this information can be tricky. You don't want to scare your clients, but you also don't want to give them the idea that it's up to them to do everything "right" so that breastfeeding will get off to a good start. So after I explain the basics of breastfeeding, I transition into a discussion of how they can be proactive in preparing for common challenges, with an emphasis on looking at breastfeeding as a conversation they will have with their baby. Using visual aids like a baby doll and a knitted breast can help reinforce teaching.

I love teaching families about prenatal expression of colostrum, hand expression, spoon feeding, and working with babies who are not yet latching. I always include instruction on reverse pressure softening, and inform them that flat nipples may just be excess fluid.

I teach them about laid-back breastfeeding but also tell them that this position may not yet work when they're in the hospital, and not to worry if it doesn't because they can always upgrade once they are home and more comfortable. And finally, I make sure they are prepared for the cluster feeding that happens on days two and three, usually right when the hospital will send them home after a vaginal birth.

Finally, I make sure to include a reminder that perinatal mood disorders can begin to manifest in pregnancy, and to take any health concerns seriously. I provide them with curated links and resources aimed at reinforcing what they've learned, and information on local breastfeeding support groups like La Leche League (and encouragement to attend prenatally).

- <u>Teaching prenatal breastfeeding classes</u>
- <u>Breastfeeding Models</u>

- <u>Prenatal Breastfeeding Education Booklet</u>
- <u>Childbirth Graphics</u>
- <u>Noodle Soup</u>

Back to Work Consults

Families are often anxious about their return to work, but including this information in a regular home visit can be overwhelming. Back to work strategy can certainly fill an entire visit, and this could become a very popular service with savvy pricing or a group offering.

When counseling families who are returning to work, take time to acknowledge their feelings around their return to work. Allow them to share the nitty gritty of their work schedule, their childcare plans, and what they're most afraid of. These sessions can make a real difference in breastfeeding outcomes through empowering breastfeeding parents and their support people in continuing to breastfeed when it's time to head back to the office (or back on the computer). Familiarize yourself with state laws and the Family and Medical Leave Act (FMLA).

- <u>Break Time for Nursing Mothers</u>
- <u>State-Level Workplace Breastfeeding Rights</u>
- <u>Know Your Rights: Federal Law and Pregnant, Post-Partum, and Breastfeeding Mothers</u>

Induced Lactation and Chestfeeding

Adoptive families, non-gestational parents, and transgender parents may approach you to support them in bringing in a milk supply under nontraditional circumstances. If you are not familiar with these practices, seek out continuing education so that you can support all families with the best possible support and information.

- When trans men choose to breastfeed – or 'chestfeed' their babies
- Tips for Transgender Breastfeeders and Their Lactation Educators
- Breastfeeding Without Birthing: A Breastfeeding Guide for Mothers through Adoption, Surrogacy, and Other Special Circumstances by Alyssa Schnell

What to Do When Things Get Tricky

Most of the time in private practice client relationships evolve along a fairly predictable trajectory. You meet, you build trust, you offer information and recommendations, and your client achieves self-efficacy in their individual infant feeding goals. But every so often you're going to have a client who challenges you and maybe even makes you question your competence as an IBCLC. A word of advance comfort—it happens to all of us sooner or later. Connecting with other IBCLCs provides reassurances and coping skills for those clients who push us to our limits.

One way clients can be challenging comes when they present with situations where we have insufficient education or training, or that fall outside of our scope of practice. Collaboration is key here—never hesitate to tell a client, "I'm going to need to do some research on this. Do you mind if I consult with my mentor, colleague, or networking group without mentioning your or your baby's identifying information?" Go find an IBCLC who knows what you don't know, and pay them for their time to train you. Shadow the ENT or oral surgeon if you're not sure you know enough about tongue ties. Ask a physician—preferably their physician—for guidance on supporting clients with medical issues. The point is that when you're faced with something you don't know, learn more. And when issues are outside of your scope of practice, don't try to fake it, refer your client to the appropriate professional.

What happens when a client is unhappy with your services? Best-case scenario is that you get an email with their complaint; worst-case scenario is that you find out about it on social media. The client may ask you for a refund or simply want to tell the world what a horrible person you are. It can be devastating to read an online review knowing how much you put into that client and be totally unable to defend yourself without compromising your client's right to privacy.

This is really just my personal opinion, but I recommend against giving refunds. Instead, consider offering a free follow-up visit to that unhappy client. Validate their feelings of frustration with you, and take the path of kindness in offering to stay with them in this journey. Resist the urge to explain yourself or challenge their assertions. This is their journey, not yours, and you'll never argue your way into changing someone's mind about their own personal experience.

Some of these unhappy parents may be struggling with perinatal mood disorders (diagnosed or otherwise), and responding with kindness may have a positive effect on the overall situation. They think they are angry with you, but when you don't take the bait but instead offer empathy, things may change for the better.

Or they may not. That bad online review may always be there, taunting you from the internet's unforgivingly long memory. Let it go. Focus on your satisfied clients and commiserate with other IBCLCs. And most of all, keep working!

- <u>5 Steps to Deal With Bad Online Reviews on Your Practice</u>
- <u>How Doctors Should Respond To Negative Online Reviews</u>
- <u>Doctors fire back at bad Yelp reviews — and reveal patients' information online</u>

Optimizing Your IBCLC Private Practice

The course of IBCLC private practice never did run smoothly, and we've all weathered both ups and downs. Some months you will be so busy that families get frustrated that you don't have time for them. Other months the phone won't ring at all and you'll wonder if it's time to look for another job. We have all been there. In order to survive and thrive as an IBCLC you will need to cultivate skills that will enable you cope consistently with the challenges that private practice will throw your way, as well as look for new opportunities to expand and grow.

As your practice grows, you'll start to identify your own personal strengths and weaknesses. You'll learn that you might be a rockstar when it comes to charting, but constantly running late to your appointments (true confessions time). Hone in on your strengths and celebrate how they've contributed to your success, and then reflect on your weaknesses and modify your practices so that you can grow and evolve.

Collaboration

Working solo doesn't necessarily mean working alone. Finding accountability partners to help you take care of yourself while taking care of your clients is a great way to avoid burnout and discover strategies to make the best use of your time. These partners don't have to be local—I have a friendship with an IBCLC in another part of our large state (NY), and the support we give each other helps mitigate some of the isolation of private practice. It's a safe space for both of us because we are not each other's direct competition. I also cultivate friendly relationships with other local IBCLCs, even though technically we are competing for business, because I believe that together we are strong.

If you find an IBCLC locally and your styles seem to click, consider starting a group practice where you both work with your clients. For the right pair (or more), a partnership can provide a built-in second opinion for tough situations, and a reliable way to provide clients with continuous care during holidays and vacations. You can also work with lactation counselors with a lesser credential, where they work for you and you supervise them, or contract with other providers like massage therapists or acupuncturists or childbirth educators to share space and pool resources—and revenue. When setting up a professional relationship, think ahead towards what happens if things don't work out, and consider having a trial period and an exit clause. Having that conversation up front and putting it in writing can help preserve a friendship if the business partnership doesn't work out.

Investigate working in a physician's office, through a nifty insurance option called "incident-to" billing. Under this structure, you are working on behalf of the physician, who can bill for coverage of services through the providers they are contracted with. The physician will need to be present (in the building, not necessarily in the room) and will need to sign off on your charts. You are still technically self-employed under this arrangement and can still have your own private practice.

There are IBCLCs doing truly innovative things in hospitals, outpatient clinics, and medical practices as independent contractors, integrating lactation care into a more holistic kind of healthcare. If you see a need in your community and believe you know how things can be better, consider if you can turn it into a paying opportunity for yourself. Don't wait for a job posting to show up on the hospital website—create your own dream job and convince the hospital to make it happen.

- The Basics of Incident-to Billing
- Incident-to billing: Clearing up the confusion
- Developing a lactation program in the physician's office
- How to Start a Group Private Practice
- Adding 1099 Contractors to Your Business

Expansion

Once your private practice is rolling merrily along, you may start wondering what else you can do with your credential, skills, and experience. Now's the time get creative and start pondering on other opportunities.

If you like to write, starting a blog is pretty straightforward. You can set up a free account on a blogging platform, use the Facebook page for your business, or add a page through your website builder if you want to start a blog. In terms of content, there are so many ways you can direct your focus—writing to parents, to other IBCLCs, to other healthcare professionals, or some combination. And don't rule out writing a book if you have something to say that nobody else has set yet—trust me, if you want to, you can. But don't share clinical information about your clients without express permission, and always keep in mind client privacy and HIPAA.

Your content can also be sent out through a mailing list. In order to avoid a possibly privacy violation or HIPAA breach, don't just send an email with all your clients' email addresses in the send field—don't even put them in the BCC field. It is far too easy to accidentally expose PHI through mass emailing. Instead, sign up with a mailing list service (MailChimp is the best known) that will manage sending and receiving. These services are not likely to be HIPAA compliant unless you use a paid service, but that just means that you need to be careful when it comes to your clients. Don't add them without their permission, because that's essentially sharing their PHI. However, if they opt-in to your mailing list voluntarily, and they know that the mailing list is not a secure clinical environment, then you are likely covered as far as HIPAA is concerned.

What kinds of mailing lists could you have? Perhaps you have one for your clients, where you share tips and content about parenting and wellness, or build a list around any focus that excites you. It can be as simple as a newsletter to a structured series of articles that go out at different times to different segments of your newsletter. For example, every new client who gets added to your mailing list (with explicit permission) gets a set of timed articles covering common issues over the first year (growth spurts, starting solids, teething, physical milestones, etch).

For the more visual-minded among you, think about creating infographics, memes, posters, and educational materials for parents and professionals. Video, app, and podcast production is another way to create valuable content that can also be a revenue stream as well as increase public awareness of lactation-related issues and promote a great understanding of the important role that breastfeeding plays in human development and improved health outcomes across all populations.

If you have an office, adding retail offerings expands your revenue potential, or you can develop an online sales site for retail products or professional services (like those linked to throughout this book). With any retail offerings, be sure that you are up-to-date on the WHO Code and implementation, and avoid any conflicts of interest that may arise.

- Rachel O'Brien's Blog
- Galactablog
- Nancy Mohbacher's You Tube
- Luna Lactation and Wellness You Tube
- Breastfeeding Medicine Podcast
- The Boob Group Podcast
- International Code of Marketing of Breast-Milk Substitutes
- The WHO Code, marketing, sponsorship, and why you should give a damn
- What's a Good HIPAA Complaint Email Marketing Service To Use?

Work-for-Hire

As your reputation as an IBCLC grows, you may discover opportunities to put your education, experience, and expertise to work as a paid consultant for corporate entities. In other words, companies may hire you to do lactation-related work for their own internal use. Some examples include:

- Creating handouts for a hospital or clinic
- Developing a corporate lactation program
- Providing your opinion on a service or product for families
- Consulting on a service or product for other IBCLCs
- Writing an article for publication

I want you to hear one thing loud and clear: if you're not going to own it, don't work on it for free. Don't let any company or hospital or doctor pick your brain without charging them for it, and don't give them anything they can sell directly or use as a marketing tool. Your knowledge and your time are worth it, and hospitals and for-profit businesses have a budget to pay you.

Agreeing on a fair price is a negotiation. You're going to ask for the maximum amount you think is appropriate, you're going to expect that they want you to work for them for next-to-nothing, and you'll meet in the middle at a fair price. Don't ever take a freelance job that will cost you money. The goal is to make money, or don't do it at all.

Don't worry, nobody is going to be offended if you ask to get paid. The worst-case scenario is that they'll say, "We don't have a budget to pay you." Then you say, "I'm so sorry this won't work out. Please come back to me if anything changes." In some cases, they may even respond by offering you something, and once they reveal that they do have a budget to pay you, let the games begin! Be firm with them on the value of what you can provide, and keep the conversation going until you either get a fair rate/fee or realize that they're never going to pay you what you're worth.

- <u>The Complete Guide to Setting and Negotiating Freelance Rates</u>
- <u>How to Negotiate Freelance Rates</u>
- <u>Never Negotiate Your Freelance Rate</u>
- <u>Having the Guts to Never Negotiate Your Freelance Rate</u>
- <u>Your Freelance Rates Are Fine—Here's How To Justify Them To Clients</u>
- <u>Get Paid What You're Worth: 37 Negotiation Tactics for Every Freelance Writer</u>

Note: some of the links in this section are on pages hosting paid products or services. I do not endorse any of them, and I don't believe you need any of these services in order to negotiate a fair rate with corporate clients.

Professional Development

Professional development encompasses everything we do to stay current on research, ethics, skills, and best practices. Continuing education credits are one way to qualify to recertify as an IBCLC, but many of us pursue continuing education above and beyond IBLCE's requirements.

And don't just get continuing education—consider providing it. Perform research, write for the Journal of Human Lactation or Clinical Lactation, put together a lecture and put it out there towards booking engagements at conferences. Put together your own conference, locally or larger.

Become a mentor to an aspiring IBCLC. Our profession will thrive only if we can grow our numbers. These students need us to be available to them, and they need quality hands-on training from experienced IBCLCs.

Finally, get involved with the local branches of professional organizations for lactation consultants, in addition to involving yourself on national and international levels. Change starts with participation; if you stay on the sidelines, you can't be a part of the conversation.

- FAQs for Recertification
- LactSpeak: Professional Speakers in Lactation
- International Lactation Consultant Association
- United States Lactation Consultant Association
- United States Breastfeeding Committee
- Journal of Human Lactation
- Clinical Lactation
- GOLD Learning
- iLactation
- USLCA Webinars
- Mentoring the Next Generation of Lactation Consultants
- Mentoring Our Future by Denise Altman
- Lactation Consultants Need to Diversify Yesterday

Advocacy

Are you passionate about making change in the world on a larger scale? Do you get angry when you read yet another op-ed about how breastfeeding isn't so great? Are you fascinated by public health? Then, please, harness your energies into breastfeeding advocacy. Be a voice for families, for babies, for diversity, for inclusivity, for science, for research, and for love.

- Kimberly Seals Allers
- Reaching Our Sisters Everywhere
- Seven Ways To Support Black Breastfeeding Week

Enjoying Your IBCLC Private Practice

You're on an incredible journey, watching new families find their way in the world. I've worked with hundreds of clients and each baby remains a brand-new miracle in the world. Here are my ten tips for enjoying this calling:

- When doing your infant exam, look into the baby's eyes and thank them for working with you
- Say yes when families offer you water
- Set boundaries that preserve your personal time
- Make a lactation friend who loves what you love and will share in your victories and frustrations
- Laugh at your own jokes
- Believe in families
- Soak up the oxytocin
- Take a break for a day, a weekend, a week, or longer
- Say "thank you" when a client or a colleague pays you a compliment
- Consider self-care a necessary work-related expense

You are making a tremendous difference in the world—I mean that from the bottom of my heart. Thank you for being an IBCLC!

ACKNOWLEDGMENTS

I cannot fully express my deep gratitude to Jen Deshaies IBCLC for being my sounding board and editor for both of my books. Her fingerprints are all throughout this book, and I feel truly blessed that our connection through La Leche League of New York developed into a true friendship. I love you, Jen!

Thanks to the entire community in my Facebook Group for Paperless Private Practice for Lactation Consultants for inspiring me with your resourcefulness and acumen. To my early readers Marcda Hilaire, Nicole Jenkins, Leah Jolly, Allyson Murphy, Katherine Morrison, Rachel O'Brien, and Stephanie Wagner, I'm grateful to you for providing feedback and encouragement to improve the book and keep me motivated.

My attorney Linda Strauss, Esquire, and editor Brian White made the book real with their professionalism and expertise. My logo by Gina Goodman and photos by Laura Vladimirova featuring Shoshana Cherson and her lovely daughter Noa made everything beautiful. My thanks and admiration to all of you.

And lastly, to IBCLCs and IBCLCs-to-be—we truly are making the world a better place, one sweet family at a time. Keep learning, stay passionate, and above all, keep bringing yourself to everything you do, because you are a gift to the world.

APPENDIX A—QUALIFYING FOR THE IBLCE EXAM

Figuring out how to become an IBCLC is often the most challenging part of the whole process. Unlike other related healthcare fields (such as clinical social work, physical and occupational therapy, speech-language pathology, and counseling), there are only a handful of established university programs that include the education component along with the clinical component in an organized and structured way. In other words, you're not likely to be able to get a master's in lactation and have your department chair help you land an internship at an outpatient lactation clinic.

IBLCE, the credentialing body for IBCLCs, requires education and clinical training in order to qualify to take the exam, and I'll explain more in an upcoming section. I highly recommend joining an online support group, such as Want to Be an IBCLC? on Facebook, which is a great resource for finding free or low-cost courses to meet the educational requirement. It can also be helpful to connect with the nearest local chapter of USLCA.

If cost is an issue for you, I have included some resources below for a handful of scholarship opportunities for meeting the educational requirements. I wish there were more.

From IBLCE:

- Candidate Information Guide: For initial, repeat and lapsed candidates who plan to apply for the IBLCE exam
- Certification FAQs
- IBLCE Credential Manager Guide for Initial Applicants

Additional Resources:

- Wondering how to become an IBCLC?
- Want to Be an IBCLC? Facebook Group
- How to Become an IBCLC
- Becoming a Lactation Consultant (You Tube)

- <u>Lactation Certification & Training Programs</u>

Scholarship opportunities:

- <u>MILCC Scholarship</u>
- <u>Health E-Learning Trudi Szallasi Memorial Scholarship</u>
- <u>UCSD Vicki Wolfram Lactation Ed. Scholarship</u>
- <u>Breastfeeding Outlook Felix Biancuzzo Memorial Scholarship</u>

Educational Requirements

Health Sciences Education

If you are not already a licensed clinical healthcare provider, you will need to supply transcripts showing college or university credits in the following areas:

- Biology
- Human Anatomy
- Human Physiology
- Infant Child Growth and Development
- Introduction to Clinical Research
- Nutrition
- Psychology or Counseling Skills or Communication Skills
- Sociology or Cultural Sensitivity or Cultural Anthropology

And these courses can be taken through continuing education or as a university level course:

- Basic Life Support
- Medical Documentation
- Medical Terminology
- Occupational Safety and Security for Health Professionals
- Professional Ethics for Health Professionals

- Universal Safety Precautions and Infection Control

Distance learning is an acceptable option, provided that the course is offered through an accredited institution. Independent study followed by a test from an accredited organization can also provide you with credits. A for-profit educational institution may be able to provide you with the courses you need; however, please be aware that there are many bad actors in this field, so it's important to research carefully.

If you are unsure whether your desired educational offering will satisfy its requirements contact IBLCE directly.

- Health Sciences Education Guide for individuals interested in becoming International Board Certified Lactation Consultants
- The Database of Accredited Postsecondary Institutions and Programs
- 5 Steps to Check if an Online Program Is Accredited
- Be Selective In Choosing A For-Profit College
- The Rise and Fall of For-Profit Schools
- Dozens of For-Profit Colleges Could Soon Close
- College Board's College Level Examination Program (CLEP)
- DSST Exams for College Credit
- Health Sciences Summary
- Health Sciences Education Guide
- Health Sciences Education

Lactation Specific Education

IBLCE requires you to show proof of completion of 90 hours of education that covers the lactation-specific areas listed in their detailed content outline. This can be done through a structured course covering all 90 hours, or piecemeal through multiple sources. It's possible to find free or low-cost Continuing Education

Recognition Points (CERPs) and as long as they are offered by an IBLCE Verified Provider, they will count. Contact IBLCE directly to check if a source is verified or if your desired educational offering will be accepted before spending any money or time.

- IBLCE IBCLC Detailed Content Outline
- Health E-Learning's Breast Ed Series
- Lactation Education Resources
- Want to be an IBCLC? Online Lactation Education

Clinical Experience

You must document and be prepared to submit proof that you have performed supervised clinical hours working with breastfeeding families, and IBLCE recognizes three pathways for obtaining those hours. Each pathway requires the educational requirements listed above.

- Lactation Specific Clinical Experience
- Lactation Specific Clinical Practice Calculator – this will download an .xls spreadsheet
- Which IBLCE Pathway is Right for Me?

Pathway One—Health Professionals and Volunteers

Pathway One is for people who are already working or volunteering in some capacity with breastfeeding families. This pathway is relatively straightforward for doctors and registered nurses; less so for paid/unpaid breastfeeding helpers.

In order for your paid/unpaid work with breastfeeding families to qualify as an "appropriate supervised setting," IBLCE requires that following elements be in place at the training source (source: Certification FAQs):

- "Provide structured training programs for their counsellors which includes comprehensive education in breastfeeding and lactation management."
- "Have a Code of Ethics or Professional Conduct."
- "Provide structured supervision for counsellors, with an appropriate level of training."
- "Provide a continuing education program for counsellors."

The FAQ states, "The following healthcare delivery settings meet this criteria and clinical hours can be earned through paid or volunteer work on an hour-for-hour basis in these settings: hospital, birth centre, community clinic, lactation care clinic/practice, primary care practitioner practice/office."

If you work with a volunteer organization on IBLCE's list, then you can get credit for your volunteer work. You get more credit for in-person work; less if you are only providing phone support, but both count. Look for your volunteer organization on the list provided by IBLCE.

Note that supervision is necessary in this pathway. You cannot set up your own breastfeeding café and get credit for that. The idea is that you are accountable to someone with a higher level of experience and qualifications who will offer you guidance as you work with families.

Remember this is a learning opportunity, and you may need to seek out opportunities to develop skills that you may not be using day-to-day. For example, if you are providing peer-to-peer breastfeeding support, you may not have the opportunity to touch breasts or babies, so you would need to locate opportunities to develop these skills. If you are an RN on a postpartum floor working with newborns before discharge, you may never have the opportunity to observe how much babies change between three days and three weeks, let alone meet a distractible four-month-old. The adage "you don't know what you don't know" is so true for this pathway. Step outside your environment to discover what else you will need to learn.

Volunteer work is, by its nature, unpaid, and some volunteer organizations may prohibit you from taking tips, stipends, or grants to help subsidize your costs. If you have a paid position in a clinical setting, a benefit of Pathway 1 is the ability to earn income while qualifying for the exam.

- <u>Pathway 1: Recognised Health Professionals & Recognised Breastfeeding Support Counsellors</u>
- <u>List of Recognised Health Professions</u>
- <u>Recognised Breastfeeding Support Counsellor Organisations</u>
- <u>Certification FAQs</u>

Pathway Two—University Degree

In Pathway Two, you are completing an academic program that includes the 90 hours of lactation-specific education and provide a supervised clinical experience totaling 300 hours. At the time of writing, IBLCE lists only a handful of programs that meet their requirements.

If you are considering a program not on this list, check with IBLCE before enrolling. IBLCE states, "Beginning January 1, 2017, academic programs purporting to prepare students to qualify for the IBLCE exam through Pathway 2 must be accredited by the <u>Commission on Accreditation of Allied Health Education Programs</u> or an equivalent accrediting body. In 2016, IBLCE extended this deadline to January 1, 2018 for Pathway 2 programs that were in the formal application process with CAAHEP, which is equivalent to having submitted the program's self-study report." A program may advertise that they train lactation consultants, and it would be so frustrating and disappointing to pay money and then find that IBLCE does not accept that program.

The primary benefit of Pathway Two is coordination between your coursework and your clinical hours. This is probably the most complete pathway. The downside is that you must physically attend the program, and relocating may not be an option for you. Scholarship funds, grants, or financial aid may be available to cover a portion or even all of your tuition and fees when you are accepted into a university program.

- Pathway 2: Accredited Academic Programs
- Birthingway College of Midwifery
- Carolina Global Breastfeeding Institute
- Drexel University
- Portland State University
- Union Institute and University
- University of California San Diego Extension

Pathway Three—Mentorship

Under Pathway Three, you are responsible for finding an appropriate IBCLC mentor or mentors to supervise the clinical portion of your training for 500 total hours. You must conform to IBLCE's guidelines, complete an online application, and pay a fee to IBLCE. You are also responsible for the educational portion, which will need to be obtained separately.

Your mentor will be required to create a plan for your mentorship that "covers all of the duties listed on the Clinical Competencies for the Practice of International Board Certified Lactation Consultants," provide you with opportunities to observe clinical work (does not count towards hours) and perform clinical work (does count towards hours), and provide a report to IBLCE. Additionally, they will oversee any other mentors you may choose to work with while acquiring skills in settings other than your mentor's primary practice setting. The mentor will also assign reading and may require you to undertake projects or take tests to evaluate progress.

As you can see, mentorship may be the most rewarding way to meet the exam requirements, but also the most challenging. You will need to live or reside in an area where you have access to an IBCLC who can serve as a primary mentor, and you must be in a practice setting where you are permitted to do hands-on work with dyads. Some mentors will charge a fee to supervise mentees; this is entirely at your discretion.

Because you will be creating this plan independent of an educational institution, financial aid and scholarships will not be accessible to you. However, look into small business grants or loans because you never know where you might find funding that may even cover education.

To find a mentor, start with your local branch of ILCA or your local breastfeeding coalition. Here is a sample letter to send to a potential mentor, which you should adapt and personalize (don't just copy):

Dear _____,

I hope this finds you well. By way of introduction, I am _____, and I am contacting you to inquire about your interest and availability in serving as my mentor under Pathway Three to qualify for the IBLCE exam.

*Include 1-2 sentences describing your background

*Include 1-2 sentences explaining your plans to obtain the required educational hours

*Include 1-2 sentences on why you have written to this particular person (if applicable)

I am available to dedicate _____ hours a week to my internship and understand that not all of those hours will count towards my supervised clinical hours. I have attached my resume.

If you are currently available to work with interns, please let me know how I may apply to work with you.

Best regards,

Your Name

If you live in an area with a lot of IBCLCs, you may be tempted to cast a wide net and just cold email every single one of them. While you may still potentially find a mentor this way, a more targeted approach is often more fruitful. A personal appeal, rather than a form letter, is more likely to trigger a response.

Don't expect an immediate response. If you don't hear back within a few days, you can send a short follow up:

Dear _____,

I reached out to you a few days ago to inquire about the possibility of interning with you to obtain my clinical hours for the IBLCE exam. If you are unavailable, would you possibly be able to recommend someone?

Many thanks for your time and consideration.

Best regards,

Your Name

If you don't hear back after that, do not take it personally. The IBCLC may be busy, she may be dealing with personal issues, or she may be on a much-needed vacation and not responding to emails. Move on to the next person and just keep trying.

From IBLCE:

- Pathway 3: Mentorship
- Pathway 3 Plan Guide: For the development and verification of Pathway 3 clinical mentorship plans

- Pathway 3 Plan Verification Online Application Manual
- Clinical Competencies for the Practice of International Board Certified Lactation Consultants (IBCLCs)

Preparing for the Exam

At the time of writing, IBLCE offers the certifying exam twice a year. You must submit an application and pay a fee by a certain date. Your clinical hours and education must be completed by the application date. Exam results are not released right away. The most current list of fees and dates can be found on the IBLCE website.

The exam is multiple-choice and administered by computer, and a portion will require the interpretation of images.

Recommended textbooks:

- Breastfeeding and Human Lactation by Karen Wambach and Jan Riordan
- The Breastfeeding Atlas by Barbara Wilson-Clay
- Counseling the Nursing Mother: A Lactation Consultant's Guide by Judith Lauwers and Anna Swisher
- Breastfeeding: A Guide for the Medical Profession by Ruth A. Lawrence, MD

Exam prep and study guides:

- IBLCE Detailed Content Outline
- Core Curriculum for Lactation Consultant Practice by ILCA – the latest edition is due out in 2018
- Lactation Exam Practice
- Breastfeeding Outlook Exam Review
- Comprehensive Lactation Consultant Exam Review by Linda J. Smith

- Test-Taking Strategies: A Guide to Taking and Passing the IBLCE Exam by Marie Biancuzzo

From IBLCE:

- Candidate Information Guide: For initial, repeat and lapsed candidates who plan to apply for the IBLCE exam
- Certification Fees & Key Dates
- Apply for the IBCLC Exam & Exam FAQs
- IBLCE Exam Admissions Policy
- IBLCE Procedures for Breastfeeding Breaks during Exam Administration
- Exam Day Tips
- Pearson VUE testing tutorial and practice exam

Recertification

Your initial certification is good for five years, and then you will need to recertify. You may choose to take the exam again, or submit proof that you have earned seventy-five Continuing Education Recognition Points (CERPs) within those five years. Every ten years after initially passing the exam you are required to take the exam again; CERPs will not be accepted.

You must submit an application to IBLCE by the appropriate deadline to prevent any lapse in certification. The most up-to-date dates and fees are posted on the IBLCE website.

CERPs can be obtained through in-person or online continuing education, or by serving as a mentor to a Pathway Three applicant. Some CERPs may be available for free or low cost, and scholarships may be available from the CERP provider.

CERPs are divided into three types, and you need to accumulate a minimum number in two of the types; the remainder can be any kind of CERP. L-CERPs cover lactation and you need at least fifty of those. E-CERPs cover ethics and you need at least five of those. R-CERPs are a catch-all for education that doesn't fit into either lactation or ethics but is still related to the IBCLC, and they can be used for up to twenty of your remaining unspecified CERPs.

From IBLCE:

- <u>Prepare for IBCLC Recertification</u>
- <u>Recertification Fees & Key Dates</u>
- <u>Apply for Recertification</u>
- <u>FAQs for Recertification</u>
- <u>Continuing Education Recognition Points</u>

Where to obtain CERPs:

- <u>Gold Learning Online Continuing Education</u>
- <u>iLactation</u>
- <u>Lactation Consultants in Private Practice</u>
- <u>How to Access FREE Continuing Education Credits as an ILCA Member</u>
- <u>USLCA Education Resources</u>
- <u>Lactation Education Resources</u>
- <u>International Consortium of Oral Ankylofrenula Professionals</u>
- <u>Professional Trainings offered by Michelle Emanuel</u>
- <u>LactSpeak</u> – see upcoming lectures listed by featured speaker
- <u>What are CERPs and do I need them?</u>

PRIVATE PRACTICE WORKBOOK

This worksheet is designed to help you keep track of key components of your private practice. A fillable version will be available on the password-protected page for this book at paperlesslactation.com/private-practice-resources using the password PAPERBACK.

What is the name of your private practice?

What is your private practice's mailing address?

What is your private practice's website?

What is your private practice's phone, fax, and email?

What is your NPI?

What is your EIN?

What is your liability insurance policy number? Include the premium amount and when you must renew.

If incorporated, list any key dates for payments and renewals, and write down where you store any corporate paperwork, along with the amounts of any planned payments.

If licensed, write down your license number and any key dates/fees for renewal.

What is your IBLCE number and what is your date of certification?

Write down when you are scheduled to recertify, and deadlines for CERP completion and submitting your recertification application. Include the payment amount for recertification fees.

If paying estimated taxes on your private practice income, list the dates that estimated taxes are due and the amount of the payments you intend to make.

Make a list of your monthly costs for private practice, and the providers you use. Not all of these may apply, and there may be some overlap.

Email:

Cloud storage:

2nd phone line:

Secure messaging platform:

EHR Platform:

Fax:

Online scheduler:

Telemedicine platform:

If you have an office, write down your address, as well as your overhead (rent, utilities, parking, etc).

If you are in-network with any insurance company, write down any important information here.

List your professional affiliations here.

If you are renting equipment, list serial numbers here.

CERP Tracker for Recertification

Use this worksheet to keep track of the CERPs accumulated towards recertification. A fillable version with formulas to help you keep a running total will be available to you on the password protected page for this book at paperlesslactation.com/private-practice-resources using the password PAPERBACK.

At the time of publication, IBCLCs can recertify by CERPS (continuing education recognition points) when their certification expires after five years. The next re-certification must be done by exam. The recertification application is due on September 30 of the year your certification expires, and all CERPs must be completed by then. The exam is offered twice a year. This information is subject to change so please check the IBLCE website for the most up-to-date recertification information.

- IBCLC Recertification
- FAQs for Recertification

My deadline to complete CERPs for recertification:

Where I keep my signed CERPs:

Running total of CERPs earned, need 75 total:
L-Cerps (lactation), need 50:

E-Cerps (ethics), need 5:

R-Cerps (related):

List the CERP provider, # of L-Cerps, # of E-Cerps, and # of R-Cerps:

www.ingramcontent.com/pod-product-compliance
Lightning Source LLC
Chambersburg PA
CBHW050514280326
41932CB00014B/2311